Kiltz's Keto is Carnivore

Kiltz's Keto is Carnivore

A Guide for a Fertile Life & Beyond

By Dr. Robert Kiltz, MD

Printed in the United States of America

First Printing, 2020

ISBN-978-1-958848-84-5 print edition
ISBN-978-1-958848-84-5 ebook edition

Waterside Productions
2055 Oxford Ave
Cardiff, CA 92007
www.waterside.com

"Civilized man is the only animal clever enough to manufacture its own food, and the only animal stupid enough to eat it."

-Barry Groves, Ph.D.

Table of Contents

This is a Wake Up Call

WE ARE SUFFERING FROM A
"HEALTHY DIET & LIFESTYLE"

Welcome to a Healthier You!

What is health & wellness and how do we achieve it? What if the theories and hypothetical stories we tell and re-tell about nutrition are mostly wrong?

We've been taught forever that sugar is the fuel for our bodies. We've made fat bad and sugar good. But is it possible that things are actually the other way around and fruits, vegetables, fibers, seeds, and nuts are harmful, even deadly? Is it possible that plants are the predators and we are the prey?

When it comes to nutrition, controlling inflammation, and fueling the human body, I know one thing to be true:

Keto is Good.
Carnivore is Best.

This is my experience as fertility specialist, scientist, and someone who progressed first to Paleo, then to Keto, and has now happily been a Carnivore for over a decade. But it's important that you figure out what lifestyle works for you, your health goals, and allows you to feel your very best.

With either lifestyle, it's not so much about WHAT you are eating, but more importantly, what you're NOT eating. It's removing the sugars and toxins, spacing out your meals, reducing or eliminating carbs, and fueling your body with what it actually needs, not just what it wants.

Today, despite medical advances, the NIH estimates that over 23 million Americans suffer from an autoimmune disease, and that number grows every year. Why the growth? Primarily diet and likely a little bit of stress and probably some environmental factors as well. The single most common symptom and cause of an autoimmune disease is inflammation. This is why any recurring intestinal troubles, ache

You are the most valuable, expensive being of the Universe. I call us the Human Ferrari, the Miracle Machine. You're in charge of YOU. You have permission to be responsible for yourself whatever your age or stage of life. Take care of who you are. This starts with deciding what goes into your mouth and what goes into your mind every single day.

You can be a grazing pig eating vegetables and grass 3-6 times a day, or a majestic lioness or mighty lion who hunts, feasts, and rests until it's time to hunt again. The choice is yours. The Carnivore Lifestyle is actually a way of simplifying what you eat and how you live.

Be mindful about what you're putting into your "bucket". Our digestive tract – what I refer to as the "bucket" – includes some of the most sensitive skin of the body. What's more, recent studies show that your brain affects your gut health, and your gut affects your brain health. Scientists have recently discovered that Parkinson's might originate in the gut and migrate to the brain and hearts of patients. I believe it is simply another inflammatory condition caused by our unhealthy diet.

Researchers studying rats saw harmful proteins make the move from the intestines to the brain. The gut and its microbes also control inflammation and make many different compounds that can affect brain health. As they say, food for thought.

Today you have the choice to change what's going on in your life and your body! The Carnivore Lifestyle will increase your blood flow, your brain flow, your reproductive flow, your bowel flow, your muscle flow, the function of your nerves, joints, your everything. Arthritis, dermatitis, bowel disorders, migraines, epilepsy, even ALS, MS, Ankylosing spondylitis (AS). So many things will be gone. If you don't believe me, start listening and learning. And do it! You'll see immediate results.

The Human Ferrari

We already are the human Ferrari. There's nothing stopping us from being a healthy, powerful machine but...

ourselves.

Dr. Kiltz giving his talk "The Human Ferrari" at TedXOCC

We seldom take the time to marvel at the incredible design and engineering of the human body. It is truly a wondrous thing. Dr. Kiltz calls it the **"human Ferrari"** because like the much-revered Italian-designed sports car, our bodies are beautiful machines designed by the **Master Creator** to do marvelous things. They are exquisite in both their design and function.

As both a physician and casual observer, it is Dr. Kiltz's opinion that we humans show more appreciation and concern for the high-priced sports car than we do for our own bodies. Why is that? We treat the sports car with kid gloves, polishing it, giving it the best gas and oil, driving it carefully and cautiously (unless on the race track). And we treat our human Ferraris with complete disregard. **We put the wrong food into our mouths, eat too much too often and in too much variety, take the wrong ideas into our minds, and we are literally wearing out our bodies with exercise and stress.**

We're treating these beautiful, expensive, irreplaceable, and amazing bodies like rental cars, or worse, Yugos, that much maligned other Italian- designed automobile that was the butt of many jokes and generally regarded as the lemon of the auto industry.

We have the ability to change all of this! We can treat our bodies like the impeccably designed and invaluable entities we are. We've seen innumerable people take control of their health by shifting to a high-fat, med to low protein, and low to no carbohydrate (CARNIVORE!!!) diet along with intermittent feasting and mindfulness. Dr. Kiltz's analogy of the human Ferrari makes another important point that **we are ALL human Ferraris.**

We ALL have nearly the same exact blueprint and high- quality parts. There's nothing stopping us from being a Healthy, Human Machine but ourselves. People love to blame genetics for everything under the sun: why they can't lose weight, why they will likely become diabetic, get arthritis, etc. but this is inaccurate.

Are You a Temple or an Amusement Park?

In 1826, Anthelme Brillat-Savarin wrote, "Dis-moi ce que tu manges, je te dirai ce que tu es." Which translates to « Tell me what you eat, and I will tell you what you are.» There's so much truth in these words and the idea that the foods we eat control our health—mental and physical. But our health goes far beyond just the meals and snacks we eat. **Good health is also a reflection of everything we put into our bodies and our minds.** Are you waking every morning and expressing gratitude for the day ahead? Or are you turning on the news and filling your mind with negativity and despair? All of the choices we make throughout the days, weeks, months, and years have a cumulative effect on your well-being.

You are born a temple. How you care for yourself determines if you remain a temple or if you move to the amusement park.

Alcohol, processed foods, sugar, carbs, and fast food . . . these are the precursors to disease, glycation, and oxidation. Stress can frequently trigger cravings for the wrong type of foods. Your body reacts to stress by increasing your respiration, blood pressure, heart rate, metabolism, and the blood flowing to your muscles. Cravings in the ancient environment were triggered by stress. The body wants calories to get and make fat for survival. We are built for fasting. (In our ancient environments, we likely often went days and (infrequently) weeks without food.)

This is our "fight-or-flight response," and it's meant to help you cope quickly with high-pressure situations. Your adrenal glands release a hormone called cortisol into your bloodstream, and cortisol increases appetite because the body is in need of energy to fight the stressor that you are facing. Research shows that stress also interferes with hunger hormones, like ghrelin, which controls your appetite. If stress is cutting into your sleep, a lack of sleep boosts your appetite even further. You crave the instant pleasure of comfort foods or the high calories, sugar, and carbs. But these choices actually further add to your stress and lead to weight gain.

Weight gain in an ancient environment where food was scarce was critical for survival. Yet in our modern existence, gaining too much weight is a hindrance.

Animal research confirms this hypothesis. By putting an unknown rat in its cage, effectively stressing the lab rat, not only will it eat more, but it also shows a stronger than normal preference for high-sugar, high-carb foods.

If you take a step back from the pantry, fridge, or drive-thru, drink a glass of water or bone broth and think deeply about why you are eating and what you are eating, it can make a big difference in your overall health, diet and strategy. Self-awareness is key, and sometimes healthy eating boils down to good planning and mind over matter.

Weight gain in an ancient environment where food was scarce was critical for survival. Yet in our modern existence, gaining too much weight is a hindrance.

Think about who you want to be, how you want to live, and how you want to feel. Are you searching for the calm and lightness of the temple or the frenetic mayhem of the amusement park? Imagine yourself as the lioness in the temple.

TEMPLE	AMUSEMENT PARK
• High fat, medium protein, low/no carb food plan	• **Carbs, sugar, processed foods,** variety & spice
• Intermittent feasting: Meals are spaced out. 1 meal + 1-2 snacks per day. Best meal is at night just before sleep/rest	• On "roller coaster" all day. Constantly eating 3-6 meals with snacks in between.
• Walking / Yoga / Tai Chi / Intentional Movement/ Creativity/ Meditation	• **High intensity exercise** (treadmill, elliptical) that creates inflammation and steals blood flow from core
• Read inspiring books; listen to positive, insightful podcasts, learning new things	• **Focus on the negative:** news headlines, gossip
• Make time for mindful meditation, deep breathing, and reflection. Be the artist.	• Repeat harmful patterns of behavior; stressed out and giving in to stress-induced cravings

Are the Government's Nutrition Recommendations Killing Us?

The U.S. Government's Dietary Guidelines encourage Americans to reduce their consumption of saturated fat based on the outdated notion that fat leads to heart disease. Influence from Big Food, Big Ag, and Big Biotech prevents any science-based changes to these guidelines from happening. **Can the government be trusted to offer trustworthy nutrition advice?** If this study is any indicator, then the answer is NO.

A major study looked at all-cause mortality and cardiovascular disease and nutrition by tracking over 135,000 people aged 35 to 70 across 18 countries from five continents. **They concluded that high carb diets are killing many of us around the world.** Those on a low fat/high carb diet had an increased risk of early death compared to those on a lower carb/higher fat diet.

If the government were to listen to the science, the advice might change by:

- Increasing the recommended daily allowance of Vitamin D to 5,000 IU per day. Vitamin D supports every organ in the body, not just bones, and many Americans are woefully deficient in it.
- Increasing saturated fat intake recommendations. Historically the claim has been an alleged link between saturated fat consumption and heart disease. However, more recent evidence shows that saturated fat is not, in fact, linked to heart disease. Rather saturated fat has been proven to have a number of health benefits, including improved cardiovascular risk factors and liver health, stronger bones, healthy lungs and brain, proper nerve signaling, and a strong immune system. Some saturated fats, such as coconut oil, are considered superfoods.
- Recommending a reduction in processed food intake rather than sodium intake. Salt plays an essential role in the human body. There has been evidence showing that reducing sodium consumption can pose health hazards. It is worth noting that most of the salt people consume comes from processed foods. Consequently, the recommendation should be revised to suggest reducing intake of processed foods rather than sodium.

Unhealthy Eating Pyramid

RECOMMENDED BY THE GOVERMENT

- Not restricting cholesterol consumption. Past reports have told Americans to avoid eating foods with more than 300 mg of cholesterol a day (about the amount in two eggs). This put eggs, butter, whole milk, and shellfish all on a watch list, but they can all be part of a healthy diet. The best research today says that dietary cholesterol is not what determines our cholesterol level since the body makes its own. And many people today have too little cholesterol rather than too much, especially since so many are on statin drugs. Both "good" and "bad" cholesterol are essential for our health. The problem with "bad" cholesterol is when it becomes oxidized. Fortunately, there is a blood test to measure it—the OX-LDL test, but very few doctors are telling their patients about this important test.

The truth is that:

POOR DIET KILLS MORE PEOPLE WORLDWIDE THAN ANY OTHER RISK FACTOR.

According to a new report from the **Global Burden of Disease Study,** bad diets are responsible for 11 million deaths worldwide. That's more than any other individual risk factor, including smoking. The U.S. has good company. Nearly every nation fails to get the right balance of nutrients. Some because, like their American counterparts, their citizens indulge in processed meats and super-sized sugary sodas, but others because they lack basic access to nutritious foods.

Even with more drugs and research, we are not getting healthier. Despite a government campaign to decrease fat consumption, obesity and chronic diseases continue to rise at alarming rates.

The 3 Keys to Optimal Health & Longevity

THE DR. KILTZ WAY

1

FATTY MEAT, NO CARB EATING

Carnivore, Carnivore, Carnivore!

2

MIND, BODY, SMILE

Walking, Yoga, Meditation, Art, Tai Chi

3

INTERMITTENT FEASTING (FASTING)

One Meal A Day

Join Kiltz's Mighty Tribe

This is a community where Ketovores, Carnivores, Fatovers, Carnicurious, and anyone/everyone can connect with one another, share ideas, learn, and stay inspired. Conversations within the community are supported by those actually eating the Keto/Carnivore Diet. Our tribe will help members to foster new relationships, build connections, share habits, and learn to become the lion within. We are here to inspire and create leaders

Sign up here:

Why Carnivore?

For decades we've been told that a plant-based diet is the ticket to health and that meat will kill you. In a world that blindly accepts these stories, the carnivore diet is as nutritionally extreme as you can get. The thing is, when we consider the historical evidence for human carnivory, the incredible abundance of nutrients (and avoidance of antinutrients and plant toxins) in a carnivore diet, along with high-quality emerging science questioning the old anti-meat studies, the carnivore diet begins to sound, not just normal, but optimal.

For the vast period of human evolution, almost none of the vegetables and fruits you see today at the grocery store were eaten or even existed, and grains are only recent additions to our diets.

And where have they gotten us? **Since the invention of agriculture, human metabolic health has taken a nosedive.** In the early centuries of agriculture, we see human brains and skeletons shrink, and periodontal disease ran rampant.

Fast-forward a few thousand years to modern life, and we see skyrocketing incidences of diabetes, heart disease, cancer, osteoporosis, along with other "diseases of civilization" linked directly to modern diet and lifestyle.

Therefore, by eliminating the foods our ancestors didn't eat and consuming only nutrient-rich animal foods, the carnivore diet may just be the most effective way to improve your overall health and wellbeing.

Study by Harvard University

2021 Carnivore Diet

Findings from 2029 Participants over 6+ months on a Carnivore Diet

100% Diabetics came off injectable medications

92% Diabetics came off insulin completely

84% Diabetics came off all oral medications

CRP Inflammatory marker decreased significantly

90% Improvement in all diseases

Average Weight Loss
20lbs

Carnivore Diet Food Pyramid

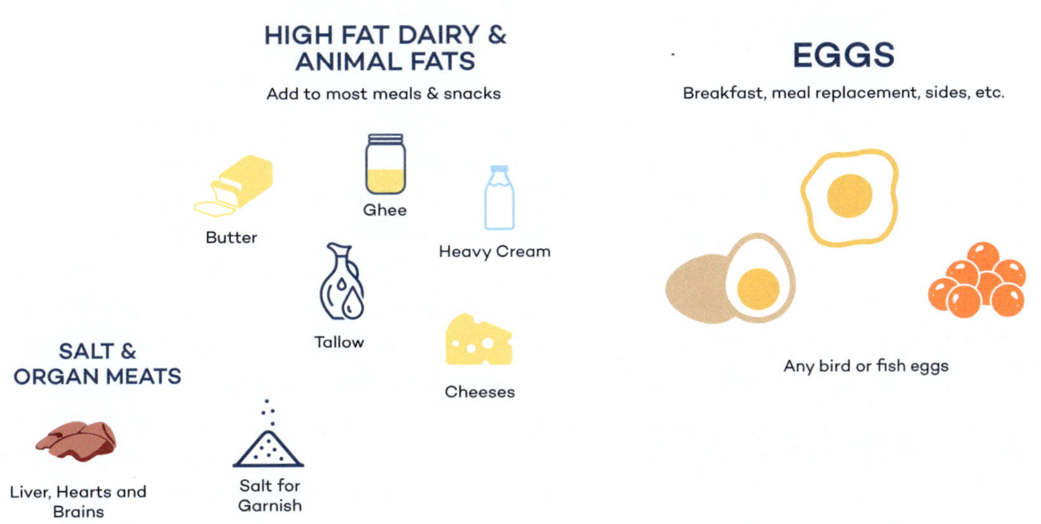

MEAT

Ideally, focus on fatty, ruminant (beef, lamb, bacon, etc) cuts of meats like ribeye, shortribs, chuck, brisket, 80/20 or fattier ground beef, etc, lamb ribs/shoulder. Use non-ruminant meats like duck, pork, chicken, and seafood for a change of pace. Dip any non-fatty cuts of meat in lots of butter.

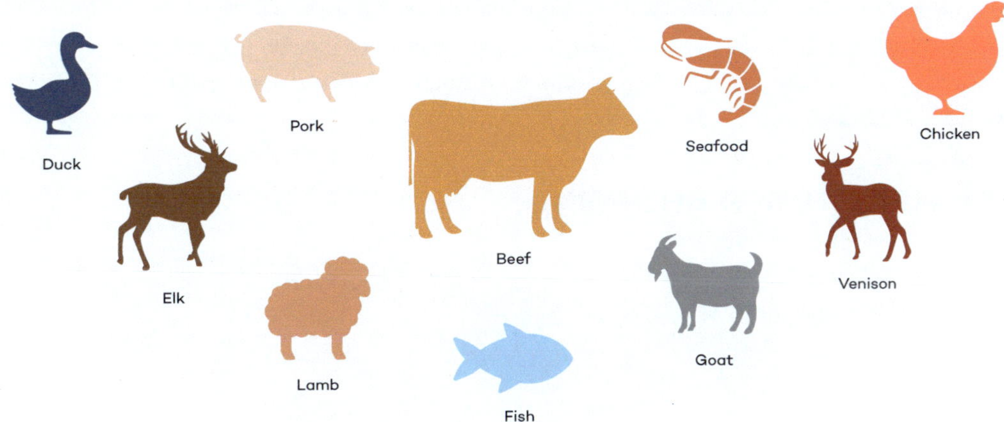

Why Carnivore?

If you're still wondering what's so special about carnivore eating that makes it preferable to other food plans, let's break it down to the basics.

IT'S NUTRIENT DENSE.

Carnivore eating sticks to the most nutrient-dense foods available to us and eliminates all of the foods that cause GI problems, inflammation, brain fog, and bloating. Nutrients are more bio-available in meats, which means your body has an easier time absorbing and using the vitamins and minerals it takes in.

IT REDUCES INFLAMMATION.

Eating an all-meat diet (and eliminating sugar and carbs) regulates circulating insulin, thereby removing the mechanisms that break down the prostaglandin inflammatory process. Carnivore eating causes the inflammatory process to turn off and on as needed, which is how it supposed to function.

IT SUPPORTS MENTAL HEALTH.

Serotonin dysfunction, low cholesterol, and zinc, DHA, Vitamin B12, iron and vitamin B6 deficiencies have all been associated with depression. The body requires amino acids, vitamins B3, B6, and B9 to make serotonin and vitamin D to release it. Because meats are nutrient-rich in all of these and have a high fat content, they can boost mood. The carnivore diet tackles nutrient deficiencies that are known to exacerbate mental health issues.

IT REDUCES CIRCULATING INSULIN.

When you're consuming sugar and carbs (both break down to glucose and fructose) three to six times a day, the pancreas is constantly releasing insulin to handle the demand (and can lead to hyperinsulinemia). On a carnivore diet, your sugar and carb intake is nominal, so there's no demand for insulin and insulin levels in your bloodstream fall giving your body a chance to rest and heal.

IT IMPROVES ENERGY LEVELS.

Inflammation and nutritional deficiencies can contribute to fatigue. Some studies have found that people with chronic fatigue have low levels of carnitine. Red meat is an abundant source of carnitine. Fat helps to fuel your cell's mitochondria. A bump in vitamin B also helps provide additional energy.

IT SIMPLIFIES MEAL TIME & SHOPPING.

There's nothing too complex about carnivore eating. Bacon, eggs, butter, beef, ice cream, salt gets it done! It's a simple and short shopping list and easy prep and cooking. There's no counting calories. That's free time you can use to do just about anything – read a book, listen to a podcast, take a walk, paint a picture, learn photography.

IT REDUCES GLUCOSE INTAKE TO NEAR ZERO.

By eliminating sugars and carbs, you reduce glucose levels and your intake of the sugars that feed glycation and glycated protein clusters call AGEs (Advance Glycation End Products).

IT IMPROVES GUT HEALTH.

Carnivore eating removes food categories that are destructive to your gut health, namely fiber, plant toxins and triggers like glutens and lectins that feed gut bacteria, irritate the delicate biome, and can lead to leaky gut.

IT CAN INCREASE WEIGHT LOSS.

Science has shown that we gain weight because our insulin levels are always elevated which cues our bodies to go into fat storage mode. And, eating processed foods throws off our ability to be satiated, therefore we keep eating to excess. Switching to a carnivore plan eliminates both of these issues. Many people begin to drop weight once they switch.

IT SUPPORTS LIBIDO & TESTOSTERONE LEVELS.

There are many studies which show that saturated fat intake correlates with increased testosterone levels. Because the carnivore diet has high intake of good-quality fats, it can help increase the testosterone levels. Additionally, the elimination of sugar, carbs, and vegetable oils also positively impacts testosterone production. Zinc, Magnesium, vitamin D, and Boron play a large role in your body chemistry and how it creates testosterone. The carnivore diet is rich in these vitamins and minerals.

IT'S GOOD FOR YOUR SKIN.

Your skin is a byproduct of what you eat. Because the carnivore diet reduces inflammation and balances insulin levels (eliminating two major acne triggers), it improves acne and other skin conditions like psoriasis and eczema.

IT SUPPORTS IMMUNE FUNCTION & HELPS PREVENT DISEASE.

Zinc, vitamin A, and vitamin D are critical nutrients for your immune system and most people are deficient in them.

IT IMPROVES SLEEP.

Sugar wrecks the quality of your sleep and increases inflammation. High sugar consumption is linked to more restless, lower quality sleep. Diabetes and hyperglycemia are also associated with insomnia. Ketones have been shown to improve REM sleep. Balanced hormones are a side effect of carnivore and hormonal balance also plays a role in sleep quality. Better sleep has a positive impact on a number of health and quality of life metrics.

IT ELIMINATES PLANT TOXINS.

When you say good bye to fruits and veggies, you also eliminate the various toxins and triggers that come along with them. Research shows that plants may not be as nutritionally beneficial as scientists once thought given their lectins, oxalates, phytates, etc.

IT PUTS YOU IN KETOSIS

Which is a good thing. Ketones, like beta- hydroxy butyrate, help to reverse inflammation. And the carnivore diet puts you into ketosis.

Fatty Meat- No Carb Eating Provides Superior Nutrition

Due to the incredible marketing efforts of various agricultural and food-processing companies, we've all been convinced that plant foods are loaded with vitamins and mineral and are the healthiest foods out there.

Truth is, fatty animal-based foods are far more nutritious and loaded with the vitamins and minerals shown to improve nearly all aspects of health, including male and female fertility.

As the graph below shows, the nutrient-density of kale and blueberries, which are widely regarded as superfoods, pales in comparison to rib-eye steak and beef liver. Combine this with the fact that kale and blueberries come packed with plant toxins and anti-nutrients, and these animal-based superfoods become a nutrient nobrainer.

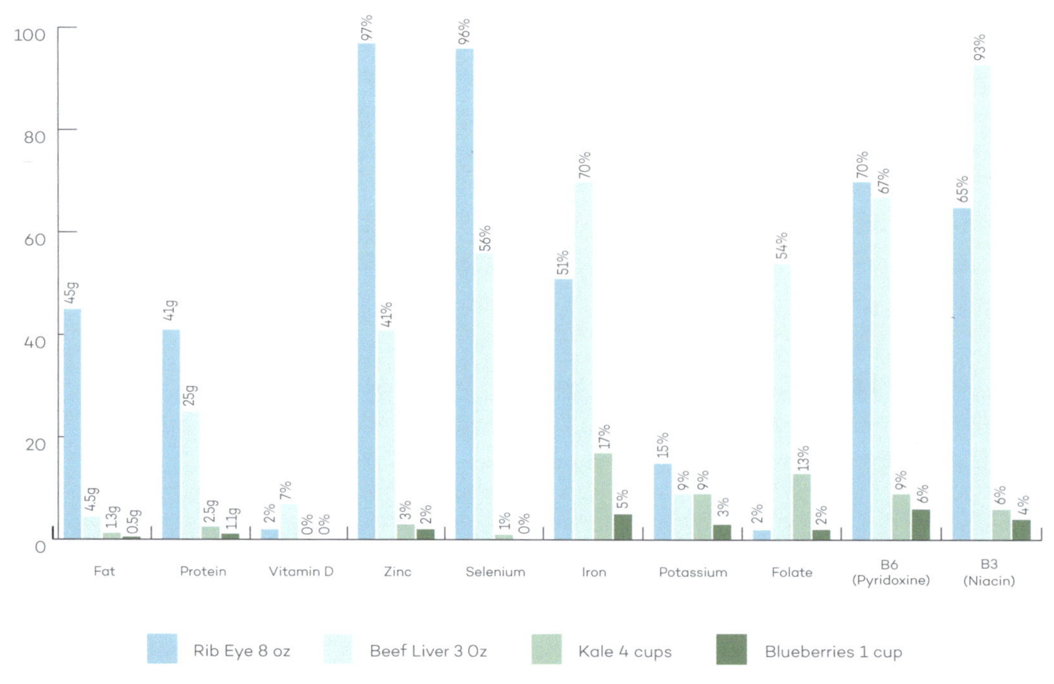

8 Nutrients Found Only in Meat

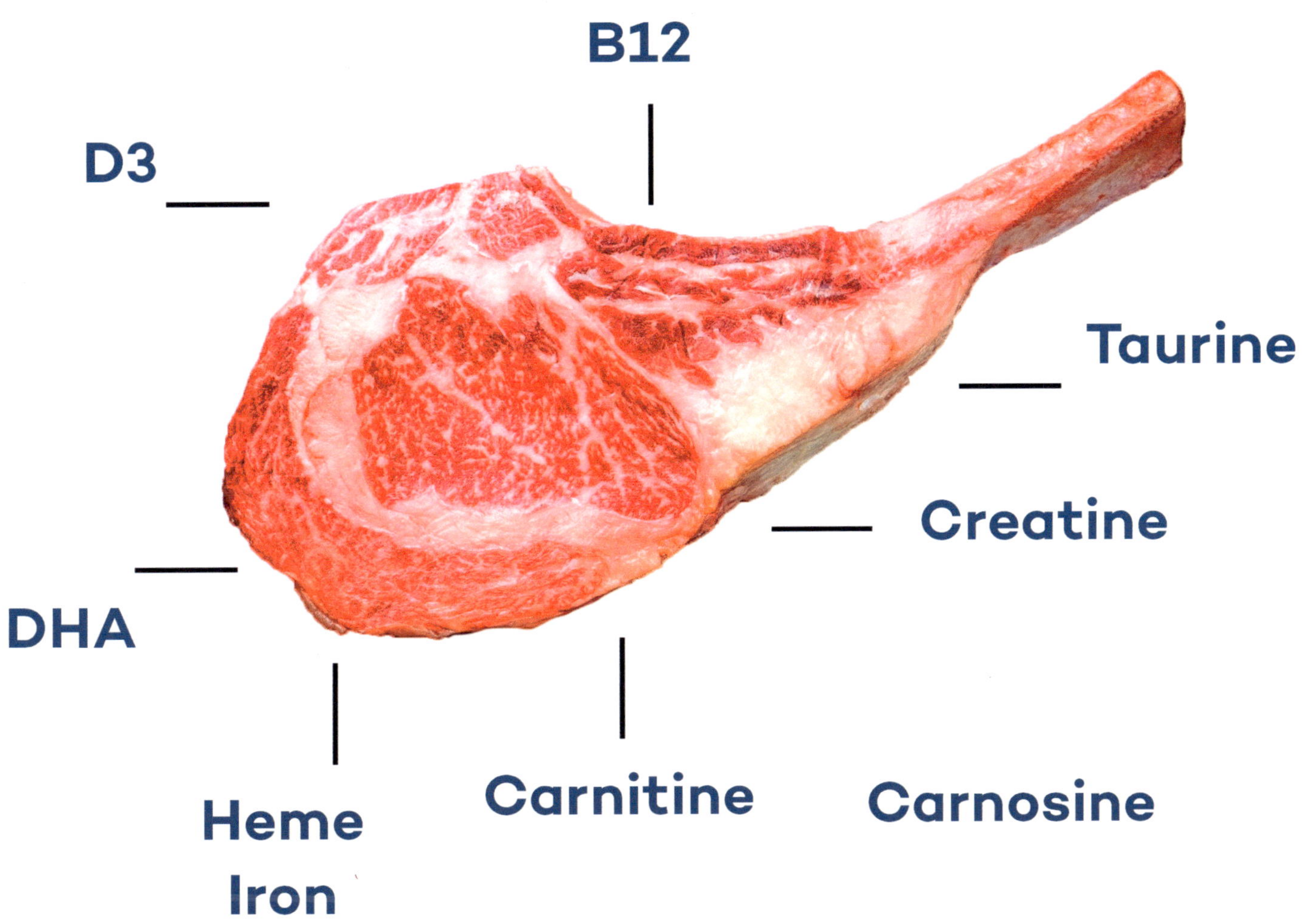

More Than Beef

Many people mistakenly believe that steak is the only acceptable food on the Carnivore Plan. Not the case. Though beef is certainly a mainstay of carnivore eating, you've got lots to choose from, including all ruminant meats (hoofed, herbivorous grazing mammals), like goat, buffalo, and lamb, plus seafood and shellfish, poultry (skin-on thighs and wings preferred), full-fat dairy, eggs, liver and other organ meats.

CARNIVORE PROTEINS

Choose humanely-raised meat and eggs and wild-caught seafood when available and affordable. Grass-fed meat is preferred if you can afford it, but the nutritional differences are slight.

Carnivore Food Options

BEEF
BUFFALO
GOAT
LAMB
PORK

WILD MEAT
BEAR
BOAR
ELK
RABBIT
VENISON

POULTRY
CHICKEN
DUCK
GAME HEN
GOOSE
OSTRICH
PORTRIDGE
PHEASANT
QUAIL
SQUAD
TURKEY

EGGS
CHICKEN EGGS
DUCK EGGS
GOOSE EGGS
OSTRICH EGGS
QUAIL EGGS

FISH
AHI/MAHI
CATFISH
HALIBUT
HERRING
MACKEREL
SALMON
SARDINES
SNAPPER
SWORDFISH
TROUT
TUNA
WALLEYE
WHITE FISH
(COD BLUEGILL)

SHELLFISH
CLAMS
CRAB
LANGOSTINO
LOBSTER
MUSSELS
OYSTERS
PRAWNS
SCALLOPS
SHRIMP
SNAILS

Super Food Nutrition Facts

Salmon

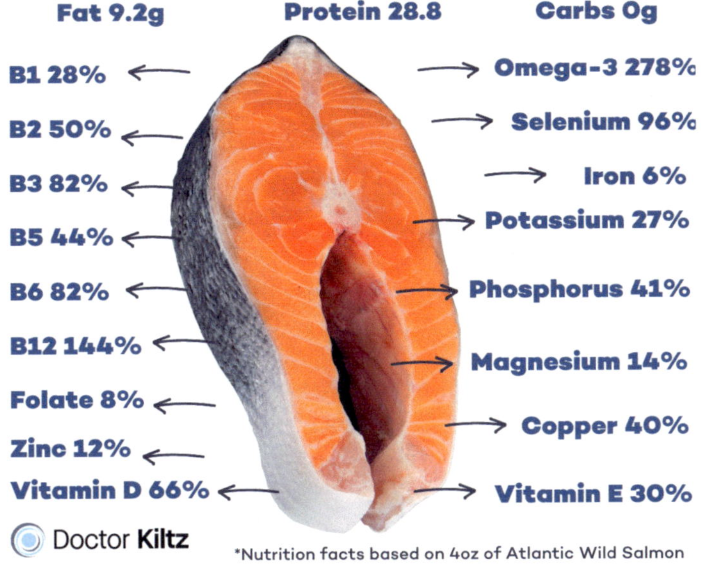

Lamb Chop Shoulder

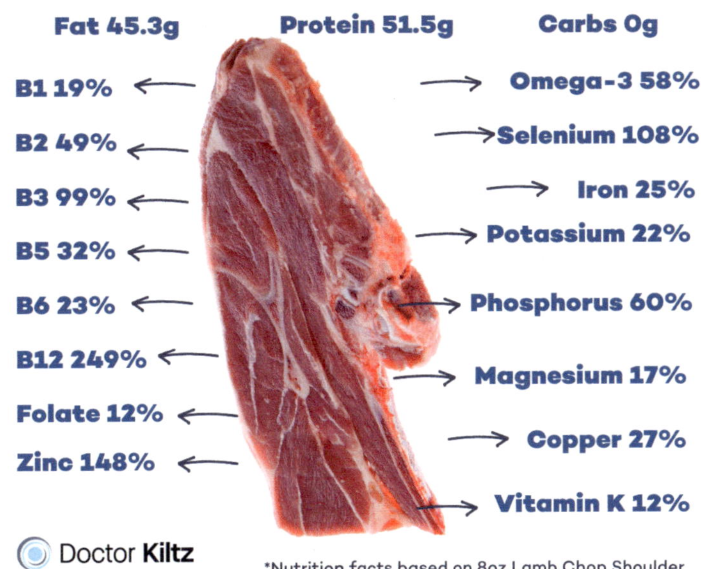

Oysters

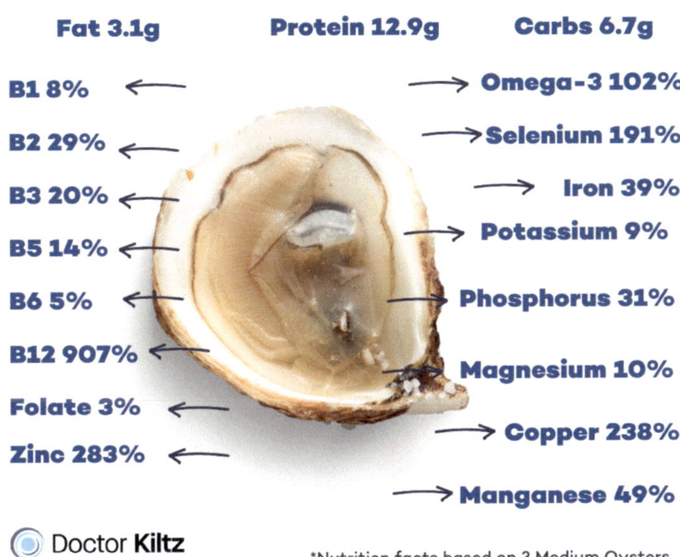

Salmon Roe

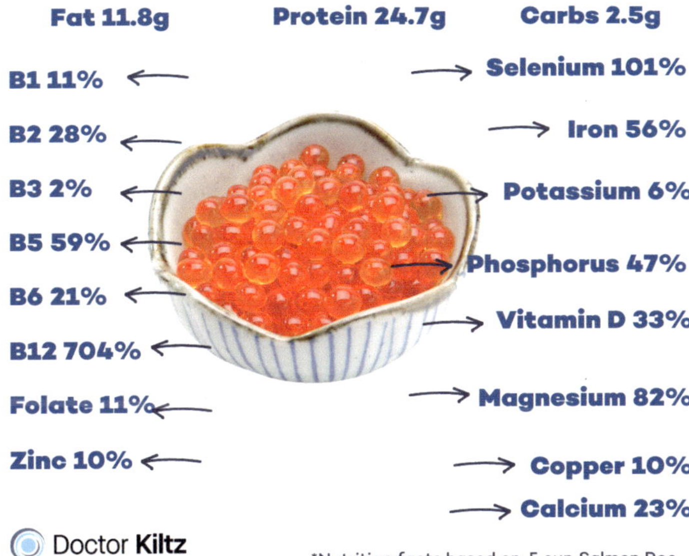

Top High Fat / Low - No Carb Foods

Crazy but True

We have never found a cave painting of a salad.

Fatty, Flavorful, and Filling

WHY RIB-EYE STEAK IS THE PERFECT CARNIVORE MEAL

I consider a rib-eye steak to be the perfect carnivore meal, and it's one I eat quite often. **Here's why:** A rib-eye steak is cut from the rib section of beef cattle. Known for their tenderness, rib-eyes also have a high fat content. Generally, the higher the grade of meat, the more fat it contains. It's half fat and half protein in a delicious package and contains no carbohydrates, sugar, or fiber.

All that beautiful marbling in a rib eye means fat—great for flavor and your body.

GENERAL NUTRITION

A 242-gram serving, or about 8.5 ounces, of grilled, boneless, choice rib eye steak with its fat trimmed contains 520 calories, 133 percent of the recommended daily intake of protein, 44 percent of the fat and 6 percent of the sodium. I recommend you don't trim the fat and eat it instead.

PROTEIN

Protein makes up about half of the calories in rib eye steak. Your body breaks proteins down into amino acids. Amino acids are essential to the creation, repair and maintenance of cells. There are three types of amino acids: nonessential, conditional, essential. Your body can produce nonessential amino acids and conditional amino acids, but may need supplemental sources in times of illness or stress. Your body cannot make essential amino acids, which come only from the food you eat. Rib eye steak offers both conditional and essential amino acids.

FAT

Fat comprises the other half of rib eye steak's calories. About 40 percent of that fat comes from saturated fat. The body needs dietary fat for energy (ATP produced in the mitochondria) and for the essential fatty acids it contains that the body can't produce. These fatty acids reduce inflammation, control blood clotting and aid in brain function. Fat also allows the body to absorb vitamins A, D, E and K.

VITAMINS

A serving of rib eye steak offers 239% of the recommended daily intake of vitamin B12 for an adult male. Vitamin B12 helps red blood cell formation, neurological health, DNA synthesis, and may play a role in reducing the risks of dementia and age-related cognitive decline. A rib eye also provides 84% of daily recommended intake of niacin, which helps in red blood cell formation, neurological function and maintaining healthy digestion, skin and nerves.

MINERALS

An 8.5-ounce serving of rib eye supplies 153% of the daily need for zinc. Zinc is integral to energy production, protein and nucleic acid synthesis, healthy immune function and cell division. The same serving of rib eye has 145% of the daily requirement for selenium. Selenium combines with proteins to form antioxidant selenoproteins that help prevent cellular damage from free radicals, which may help lower cancer and heart disease risks. Selenium may also play a role in alleviating arthritis.

“Fat is everywhere
because it’s needed
everywhere.”

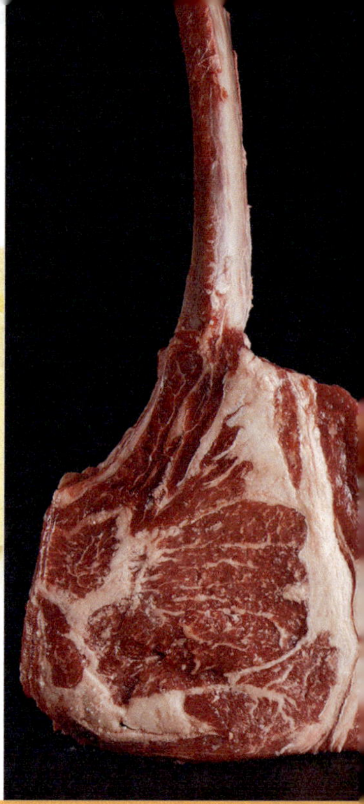

The B.E.B.B.I.S. ~~Diet~~ Way

What is the B.E.B.B.I.S. Diet?

Pronounced "BABIES", **the B.E.B.B.I.S. Diet is a high fat (80%), medium protein (20%), zero carbohydrate** food plan that focuses on bacon, eggs, butter, beef (or other fatty meat), Kiltz's full-fat ice cream on occasion, and salt. It's also referred to as The Lion King Plan or the Carnivore Plan, because you're eating like the king of the jungle—high fat, a small amount of protein, and no carbohydrates. This means eliminating all fruits and vegetables as well, as they are carbs and contain sugar and phytochemicals.

In combination with intermittent feasting, **the B.E.B.B.I.S. Diet has been shown to help boost fertility in both men and women** by naturally reducing inflammation throughout the body.

Why B.E.B.B.I.S.?

Diet is the number one source of chronic inflammation and fertility dysfunction. Making changes to what, when, and how frequently you eat can heal your body and reduce inflammation.

The excessive and repeated consumption of carbohydrates, sugars, grains, fruits, fiber and vegetables is very inflammatory to our bodies. Constant sugar in the bloodstream, along with plant phytochemicals and antigens cause an immunologic response. White cells and cytokines are enhanced. You might feel it in your joints, your skin, bowels, head, eyes, or you may not even feel it at all. Heat in the gut and bowels carries over to the reproductive organs in both men and women damaging the uterus, tubes, and testes. Untreated, chronic inflammation can result in repetitive pregnancy loss, failed implantation during IUI, IVF or natural cycle, or simply not conceiving.

Fat is essential... Plants are NOT! (All Sugar)

Contrary to what we've been told and what many of us believe, fat is healing. Fat is the building block of every cell in our bodies. Fat can reduce inflammation and help our body repair itself. It's really fruits, fibers, vegetables, grains and the constant ingestion of carbs that make us fat and chronically inflamed.

Our bodies require fat for energy. If we can't eat fat or make fat, we die. The mitochondria of our cells need saturated fat (beef fat, pork fat, butter fat). Unfortunately, the majority of fat we consume is industrial, man-made fat. What we really need to be eating is nature's fat—that stuff that surrounds the animal or is intertwined and marbled in every nook and cranny of the meat.

Excessive sugar leads to inflammation. All carbohydrates and all plant material (that's fruits, veggies, and fiber) convert to sugar and then to fat in the liver. Carbohydrates and sugar are non-essential nutrients. **Our bodies require zero carbs and zero sugar.**

Eating fat in its purest form is the simplest energy source for our bodies.

The B.E.B.B.I.S. Diet

Bacon

Eggs

Butter

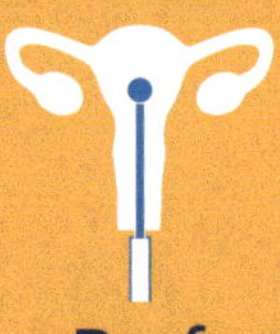
Beef

Ice Cream

Salt

WHAT TO EAT

Beyond bacon, eggs, butter, beef, Kiltz's full-fat ice cream (as a treat from time to time), and salt. I recommend that you stay very narrow in your selection of foods. Minimize the variety and simplify your meals. **Eliminate pasta, bread, yogurt, milk, seeds, and nuts.** Stay away from lean meats and try to choose grass-fed, all-natural meats. B.E.B.B.I.S. is about streamlining and simplifying.

You want to consume fatty meats like a rib-eye steak, not lean, fat-free chicken breast. You need to eat the fat. By adding fat, cream, butter, and eggs, you reduce inflammation; you reduce your appetite; you reduce your glucose levels; your energy is so much better; and your body begins to heal itself.

Fat in its best and purest, most natural form comes from animals (lard, tallow, butter, ghee, duck fat). Secondarily, there are several fruits and vegetables that are high in fat, like coconut oil, cocoa butter, and hemp seed oil. Stay away from vegetable oils like soybean, canola, vegetable, sunflower, and corn oil.

Be sure to include enough salt in your diet. Your body needs salt to help regulate fluid balances. As you're eating fewer processed foods and your body begins to shed electrolytes and fluids while in ketosis, your body also loses salt. Even transitioning from regular keto to the **B.E.B.B.I.S. Diet,** you will lose extra water from inflammation. Brain fog, muscle cramps, headaches, dizziness, and similar symptoms are all likely signs you need more salt.

Good Meal Choices:

- Rib Eye Steak or other cut with good marbling
- Pork Belly
- Liver/organ meats
- Pork/Lamb Shoulder, Chops, Ribs, Brisket
- Skin-on Chicken thighs and wings fried in own fat

HOW MUCH TO EAT

What you eat is far more important than how much you eat. You will find that fatty meats are more filling than lean meats, and you will likely feel full before you finish your meal.

WHEN TO EAT

Once per day is best. Intermittent fasting (or intermittent "feasting" as I refer to it) is highly recommended with the **B.E.B.B.I.S. Diet.** This involves eating just one meal a day and allowing 12-24 hours between feedings. **We're not meant to eat 3-6 meals a day with snacks in between,** constantly filling the gut with fiber and carbs that ferment and feed the bacteria and yeast in our gastrointestinal tract causing more disease. Our bodies are well-designed to go without food, yet most of us consume excessive calories that add fat to our bodies. It's best to eat just before bedtime, giving your body time to rest and digest while you sleep.

WHAT TO DRINK: Water, Coffee, Tea, Bone Broth

Have a cup of coffee or tea with cream or butter and a glass of water (still or bubbly with no added sugar) when you need it. **Avoid alcohol in all forms.** Alcohol is toxic to your body. Purchased or homemade **bone broth** is another great addition. It's a great snack and a soothing way to start or end the day.

EXERCISE

Intentional movement is key, but avoid excessive exercise. Activities like high intensity running or spin class create additional friction, heat, trauma, and damage in the body. We are meant to walk, take in the sites, not run or churn away on the elliptical. Yoga and Tai Chi are ideal options. Slow movements accompanied by mediation and quiet thinking are great for your mind, body, and soul. I urge clients to slow it down. That doesn't mean stop moving, but be cognizant that strenuous exercise heats up the body and takes the blood flow away from your core where it's needed.

Bacon, Eggs, Butter, Beef, Intermittent Feasting, Ice Cream, Salt

Eating a meat-based or carnivorous diet provides all of the essential nutrients your body needs. A vegetarian diet—even with "super foods" and their antioxidants—cannot deliver some of these essential vitamins and minerals. This is why most vegetarians must take supplements.

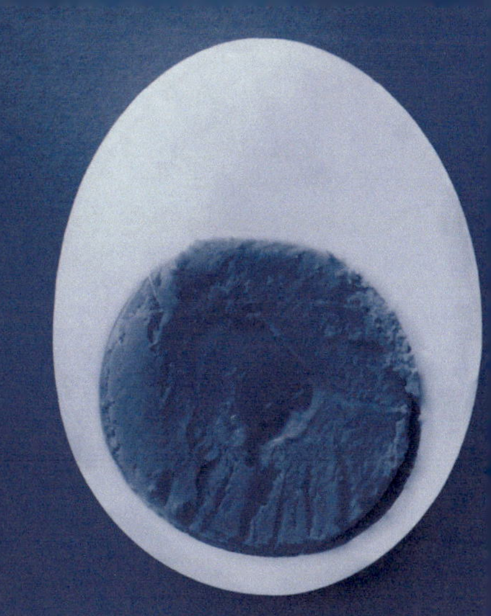

Getting Started on the B.E.B.B.I.S. Diet

- **GET RID OF ALL SUGAR (AKA PLANTS)**
- **GET RID OF ALL GRAINS** —(All plants - wheat, corn, rice, oats, etc.)
- **GET RID OF ALL HYDROGENATED OILS (AKA VEGETABLE OILS)**—Most vegetable oils contain Polyunsaturated Fatty Acids (PUFAs) and are very inflammatory
- **GET RID OF ALL FRUITS, VEGETABLES, AND FIBER (PLANTS)**
- **ADD THE FAT!** Add full-fat heavy cream to your coffee. Eat rib-eye steak, fatty bacon, eggs, and butter. Don't trim the fat, eat it!
- **PRACTICE INTERMITTENT FEASTING** — (1 meal per day and 1-2 snacks) Intermittent feasting or longer periods of fasting reduce glucose in the blood stream and reduce glycation.

Helpful Resources:

DoctorKiltz.com
Dietdoctor.com
Livinlavidalowcarb.com
Kendberrymd.com
Carnivoreaurelius.com
Kevinstock.io
Shawn-baker.com
Mariamindbodyhealth.com

Health Conditions That May Benefit from a High-Fat Low-Carb Diet

- Hypertension
- Diabetes
- Crohn's Disease
- Irritable Bowel Syndrome
- Anxiety
- Depression
- Polycystic Ovarian Syndrome (PCOS)
- Colitis
- Asthma
- Migraine Headaches
- Dementia
- Infertility
- Multiple Sclerosis (MS)
- Epilepsy
- Metabolic Syndrome
- Some Cancers
- Autism
- Parkinson's Disease
- Alzheimer's Disease
- Nonalcoholic Fatty Liver Disease

Foods to Eat on the B.E.B.B.I.S. Diet

Common Staple Meal	**Ruminant**	**Poultry**	**Fish**	**Seafood**	**Wild**
Beef	Beef	Chicken	Salmon	Oysters	Elk
Lamb	Bison	Duck	Halibut	Shrimp	Moose
Pork	Goat	Goose	Mahi Mahi	Lobster	Venison
Chicken	Lamb	Game Hen	Trout	Langostino	Antelope
	Moose	Turkey	Tuna	Mussels	Bear
	Elk	Quail	Cod	Scallops	Rabbit
	Deer	Pheasant	Sardines	Crab	Boar
	Water Buffalo		Anchovies	Clams	Rattlesnake
			Mackarel	Snail	Kangaroo

Eggs	**Fats**	**Dairy**	**Organs**	**Spices**	**Drinks**
Chicken Eggs	Tallow	Butter	Liver	Salt	Water
Duck Eggs	Lard	Ghee	Heart	Pepper	Coffee
Goose Eggs	Butter	Cream	Brain	Other Spices	Tea
Ostrich Eggs	Ghee	Creme Fraiche	Kidney		Whole Milk
Quail Eggs	Duck Fat	Cheese	Sweet Breads		Cream
	Cream	Full-Fat	Pancreas		Bone Broth
		Yoghurt	Tongue		
			Tripe		
			Bone Marrow		
			Testicals		

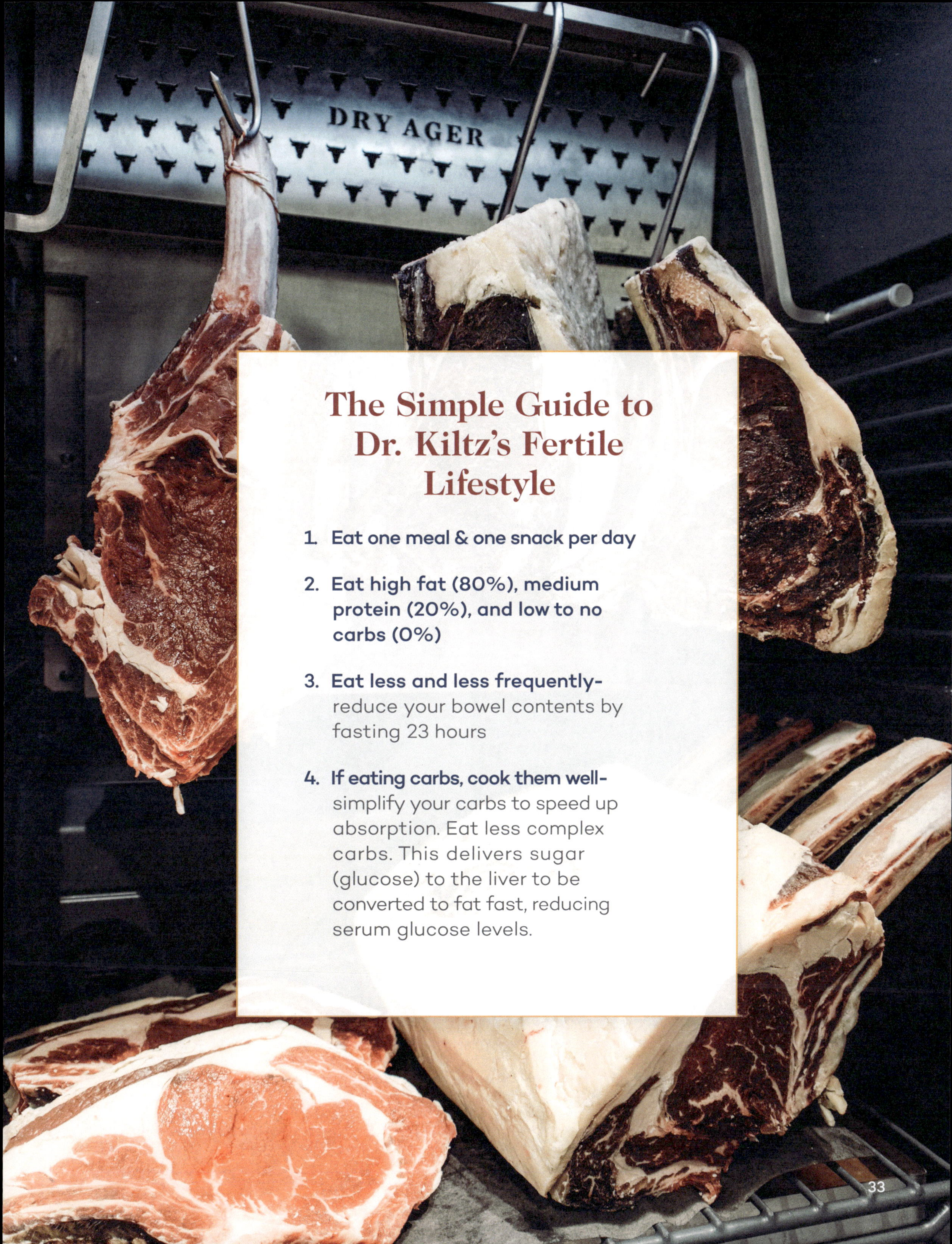

The Simple Guide to Dr. Kiltz's Fertile Lifestyle

1. **Eat one meal & one snack per day**
2. **Eat high fat (80%), medium protein (20%), and low to no carbs (0%)**
3. **Eat less and less frequently-** reduce your bowel contents by fasting 23 hours
4. **If eating carbs, cook them well-** simplify your carbs to speed up absorption. Eat less complex carbs. This delivers sugar (glucose) to the liver to be converted to fat fast, reducing serum glucose levels.

Which One Are You?

You are a Lioness/Lion

The basis of Dr. Kiltz's Carnivore Lifestyle is eating like a lioness/lion—like the queen/king of the jungle, not like a pig or other herbivore that grazes throughout the day, eating 3-6 meals filled with grass, grain, fruits, vegetables, and fiber—the very things that inflames our bodies (and it's all sugar).

What do I mean by like a lion/lioness? Simply put: eating less frequently, resting more, and digesting better, and this is all possible if you're a vegan, vegetarian, Mediterranean, Paleo, or Carnivore eater.

Eat one meal, one snack, and take one nap per day, but take infinite moments for mindful meditation throughout the day.

You need to reduce your G.I. contents by allowing the food to be digested and internalized so your body can convert the glucose and amino acids to fat and protein stores.

Pursue purposeful activities like walking, stretching, yoga, or Tai Chi, but not intense, repetitive exercise activities that create friction and heat.

Most early humans lived amidst an abundance of wild game and food sources so there was no need to ration food, nor incentive to figure out how to preserve it. A hunt meant a feast where everything was eaten. Once the food was devoured, they hunted and gathered again. Acquiring food generally took place in the early part of the day, which meant that people didn't eat until later. The time between feasts marked periods of intermittent fasting.

Over hundreds of thousands of years of human evolution, the men and women whose brains and bodies functioned the best in fasted states were the best at hunting and gathering food, and therefore the best at surviving and reproducing.

"We came out of the trees not to eat the grass, but to eat the grass eaters. It's hard to kill a cow, but easy to kill kale or corn!"

Kiltz's Carnivore Kitchen

HERE'S WHAT DR. KILTZ IS EATING FOR DINNER

Salmon

Rib eye steak

Salami & Cheese- Great Snack!

Inside Kiltz's Fridge

Steak

Pork Belly

Chicken Thighs

Deviled Eggs

Steak and Butter

Steak and Eggs

Dr. Kiltz in his Kitchen

Ribeye Steak with Blue Cheese, Butter & Foie Gras (Eat often)

SERVINGS: 2-3

INGREDIENTS

 20 oz. Bone-in Ribeye Steak

 4-6 oz. piece of Foie Gras

 4-5 Tablespoons of Butter

 2-3 Tablespoons of Blue Cheese or Gorgonzola

 Redmond's Real Salt or Maldon Sea Salt (season generously)

DIRECTIONS

- Season a room-temperature ribeye generously with salt before cooking. Grill, pan sear, or broil the steak to your desired doneness. Add butter to pan if pan searing.
- Pour fat from pan onto steak
- Sprinkle with flaky salt just before serving
- Combine 50/50 blue cheese and butter in a small stainless seal pot and melt on stove. You can combine in glass bowl and microwave as well.
- Pan sear foie gras for 30 seconds to 1 minute on each side, sprinkle with flaky salt. Serve with ribeye.
- Dip cooked steak in blue cheese butter and enjoy

French Fries

Fried in Wagyu Tallow or Duck Fat

 Eat rarely (2-6 times per year)

SERVINGS: 4

INGREDIENTS

 4 large Russet potatoes, peeled and cut into ¼-1/2 inch strips

 2 cups Duck fat (Beef tallow or lard can be used as well)

 Redmond's Real Salt or Maldon Sea Salt (to taste)

 Sour Cream for Dipping

NUTRITION

Serving Size about 1/2 cup or 1 large scoop

Food	Calories	Fat (g)	Protein (g)	Carbs (g)
French Fries	360	17	6	48

DIRECTIONS

- Cut French fries and soak in cold water for at least 1 hour, better 8 hours, ideally 24 hours
- Fill large pot with duck fat, tallow, or lard (less than 50% full to avoid hot oil from spilling over during frying) and heat to 325 degrees
- Remove potatoes from the water and pat dry to remove excess water.
- Add potatoes to hot oil with at least 1-inch of oil above the potatoes and par cook until potatoes are tannish/very light brown, usually around 5 to 10 minutes.
- Remove potatoes and place on cooling rack or into a paper bag to remove excess oil and let drain on rack. Repeat until all of the potatoes are par cooked.
- Heat oil to 350 degrees
- Add potatoes back to oil in similar size batches and cook for 2-5 minutes until golden brown
- Put fries back on cooling rack or paper bag and season with salt

Kiltz's Full-Fat Ice Cream

With a high-fat, low-carb lifestyle, even "treats" are full fat, that includes my guilt-free ice cream which can be enjoyed from time to time. Yes, there's a little bit of sugar in there, but that small amount of pure cane sugar in that much heavy cream isn't a concern. **This is the most delicious ice cream you can imagine and it's packed with all of that healthy fat your body needs.**

SERVING SIZE: About 1/2 cup or 1 large scoop.

INGREDIENTS

1 Pint of Heavy Cream (ideally locally sourced and grass-fed)

1 whole egg (or 5 egg yolks)

1 vanilla bean pod (or 1 tbsp vanilla bean paste/vanilla extract)

1-2 tbsp of sugar **(optional not required)** or honey/maple syrup/ or alternative sweetener

1-3 pinches of salt- optional and to taste

DIRECTIONS

Shake cream and pour into a large bowl. Add sugar and egg. Split vanilla bean(s) lengthwise and scrape the tiny seeds from inside the bean using the edge of a knife. For maximum flavor, steep the bean and seeds in the cream mixture for about 10 minutes. Remove the bean pod(s). Whisk until well combined and frothy. Pour into an ice cream machine and follow the manufacturer's instructions.

NOTE

Recipe can be doubled depending on the capacity of your ice cream maker.

NUTRITION-NO SUGAR

Supercharged recipe with 5 egg yolks

Food	Carbs (g)	Fat (g)	Protein (g)
Ice Cream	4.0	48.6	6.7

NUTRITION-WITH SUGAR

Standard recipe with 1 whole egg, 1 T of sugar

Food	Carbs	Fat (g)	Protein (g)
Ice Cream w/ sugar	6.5	44.1	4.9

What Does the Body Require?

AIR, WATER, FAT, AND AMINO ACIDS

That's it. We require no carbohydrates. We need a constant supply of oxygen; a little bit of water; and either fat stores or fat (animal fat) to eat. The fact that a hiker lost in the woods can survive for weeks and even months without food and just a water bottle that can be refilled from melting snow or a clean river is not an anomaly. It's by design.

Our DNA was raised on keto. Like our early ancestors, we're meant to get fat for survival, but the world we live in has changed. Prior to the development of large-scale agriculture and industrialized foods, early man's eating patterns were far different from how we eat today. Hunters and gatherers ate when they could find berries or kill a deer, and then they fasted (not necessarily by choice) until they could hunt and gather again. Depending on the season and resources, early man could go days and weeks between meals. Now with grocery stores and fast food available on every corner, it's difficult to fight the primal urge to refuel often and to excess.

The human body was built for survival, requiring fat and some protein to provide the energy needed to bear the elements and go about the necessary functions of the day. We have the potential to eliminate our biggest health problems and concerns —including issues of fertility—by going back to a basic diet, the one man first followed when he hunted and gathered the earth for sustenance.

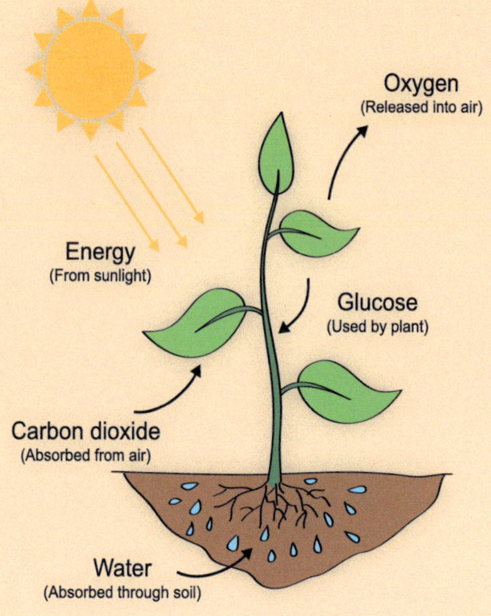

ALL CARBOHYDRATES ARE SUGAR!

Food can be classified into three major categories: carbs, protein, and fat. This is it. There's nothing else. Out of all of the plants and animals we eat, these are the three macromolecules. Surprisingly, our body requires zero carbohydrates. There are no essential carbohydrates in the universe, but fatty acids and amino acids are essential to our health and wellness. Just to be clear, the body does <u>not</u> require carbohydrates/sugar to be consumed EVER!

WHAT'S A CARB?

Carbon dioxide in the air plus sunlight and water make plants. This is the process that builds trees, vines, leaves, fruits, and roots (fiber). Most of us believe these to be "healthy" carbs, but in fact, our body can't tell the difference between a candy bar and an apple. Carbs and sugars have a very similar chemical makeup and get processed in the body the same way. **Every carb we eat is eventually broken down into sugar.**

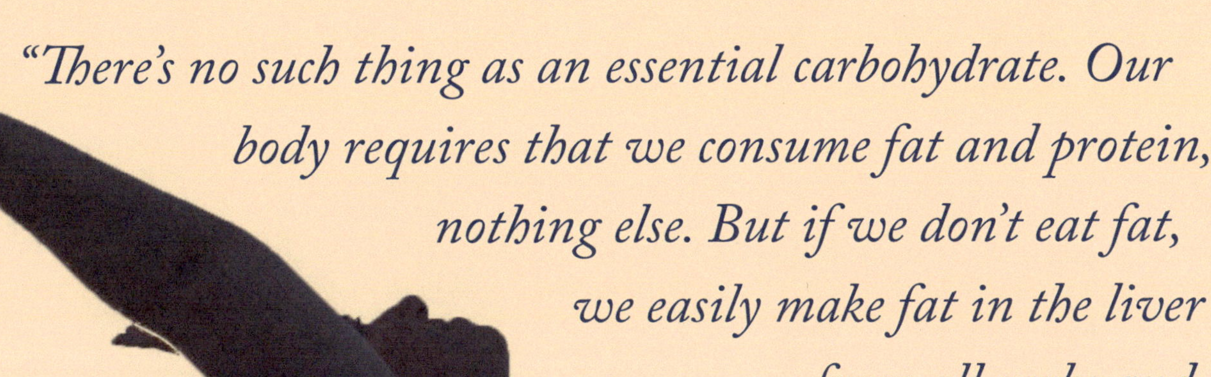

"There's no such thing as an essential carbohydrate. Our body requires that we consume fat and protein, nothing else. But if we don't eat fat, we easily make fat in the liver from all carbs and proteins."

Essential Nutrients:

Amino Acids
Fatty Acids
Minerals
Vitamins

NATURE'S TOILET PAPER
= Lettuce Highly contaminated with bacteria and yeast and causes disease. Also breaks down to simple sugars.

Why We Need Fat

FAT IS HEALING. FAT IS THE BUILDING BLOCK OF EVERY CELL IN OUR BODIES. FAT CAN REDUCE INFLAMMATION AND HELP OUR BODY TO REPAIR ITSELF.

Our bodies are made of mostly fat—lipoproteins—and require fat for the survival, growth, and the reproduction of cells. Cells require fat as fuel. In order to be used as energy, all food must first be converted into fat in the liver. **Without fat, we die.** All carbs and all amino acids (amino acids come from protein) must be converted into fat in order to be utilized as energy. Everything we consume—proteins, carbs, sugars, fruits, vegetables, fiber—must go from the stomach, to the liver, where they are converted into fat in the form of Acetyl CoA, which is the energy for the mitochondria that will then make ATP (Adenosine triphosphate) in order to maintain the body's cellular function and structure.

"We are built to get fat."

You do not convert the fat to sugar and then burn the sugar as energy. You convert all sugar into fat in the liver. When you eat fat, it does not go to the liver. It goes directly to the lymphatics to be distributed via the heart to every cell, nook and cranny of your body. It can be stored, so you can go days, if not weeks, without food. Your body was designed to store fat in anticipation of a famine that, in our present day, is not likely to happen.

The common misconception that is perpetuated by doctors and nutritionists everywhere is that fat is the enemy of a heart-healthy diet. **Saturated fats are not the enemy,** and they play a vital role in our body chemistry and total body health.

1. **Our bodies are made of fat.** Saturated fatty acids make up around 50% of our cell membranes. Fat is what creates the necessary stiffness and integrity in cell walls.
2. **Bone health depends upon fat.** In order for calcium to be effectively incorporated into our skeletal structure, it's necessary that at least 50% of our dietary fat intake be saturated.
3. **Saturated fats help protect the liver from alcohol and other toxins,** such as Tylenol and metals.
4. **Saturated fats help our immune system** to function correctly.
5. **Saturated fats have antimicrobial properties** that help protect us from harmful microorganisms in the digestive tract.
6. **A number of vitamins – A, D, E, and K,** for example—must have fat to disolve so your body can absorb them,

Eating a high-fat, medium protein, low-to-no carbohydrate diet helps improve and regulate your reproductive hormones.

A High-Fat Diet Supports Hormone Balance, Synthesis, and Function

Eating a high-fat low carbohydrate diet helps improve and regulate your reproductive hormones.

How it balances and regulates reproductive hormones generally falls into three categories:

- provides your body with the building blocks of hormones (aka cholesterol)
- reduces the intake of foods that mimic reproductive hormones
- reduces the effects of metabolic syndrome (aka PCOS) by lowering blood glucose levels

HORMONE SYNTHESIS

If you remember back to your high school or college science classes, you may remember a thing or two about hormone synthesis.

Long story short, several of the most important reproductive hormones, including estrogen, progesterone, and testosterone, are all derived from cholesterol. Cholesterol is also essential for our bodies to synthesize vitamin D from sunlight. Vitamin D has been shown to help support fertility health.

HORMONE DISTURBANCES VIA PHYTOMIMICRY OF REPRODUCTIVE HORMONES

While the link between soy and decreased fertility in both men and women has long been firmly established due to its estrogenic activity (it contains estrogen-like chemicals that bind with human estrogen receptors and interfere with normal hormonal signaling), there are over 300 plants with known estrogenic activity.

Flaxseed, sesame seeds, berries, oats, wheat, barley, dried beans, lentils, rice, alfalfa, rye, apples, carrots, garlic, and more all contain phytoestrogen.

Why exactly do plants make these hormones? Well, it is hypothesized that plans make them for the exact reason of decreasing the fertility and thus local population of the animals that eat them.

As mentioned previously, we often forget that plants are living creatures that are designed for survival, and this is one way in which plants lower populations of animals that like to eat them.

HORMONE REGULATION VIA BLOOD SUGAR AND INSULIN LEVELS

PCOS is a hormonal disorder in females that affects 1 in 10 women. It is largely characterized by the presence of high male hormone levels (hyperandrogenism) and infrequent ovulation.

Notably, PCOS is the leading diagnosis of infertility. While the exact cause of PCOS is still debated in the medical community, the story is becoming more and more clear. PCOS is highly correlated with carrying excess weight, Type 2 diabetes, previous gestational diabetes, and cholesterol problems – **problems that are all linked to high insulin levels.**

It turns out that hyperinsulinemia can cause the ovaries to make testosterone and create other hormonal imbalances that reduce ovulation frequency and influence other PCOS symptoms.

Because insulin is released after eating a high carbohydrate meal, **eating a low-carb diet is one of the most effective ways to reduce insulin levels,** and has been shown to have a favorable impact on metabolic syndromes like PCOS.

The results are so promising that one recent study showed that every PCOS patient enrolled in a High Fat Low Carbohydrate fertility diet resumed regular menstruation and ovulation and half got pregnant naturally without the need for any medical intervention like ovulation induction, IUI, or IVF.

Eating a high-fat low carbohydrate diet helps improve and regulate your reproductive hormones.

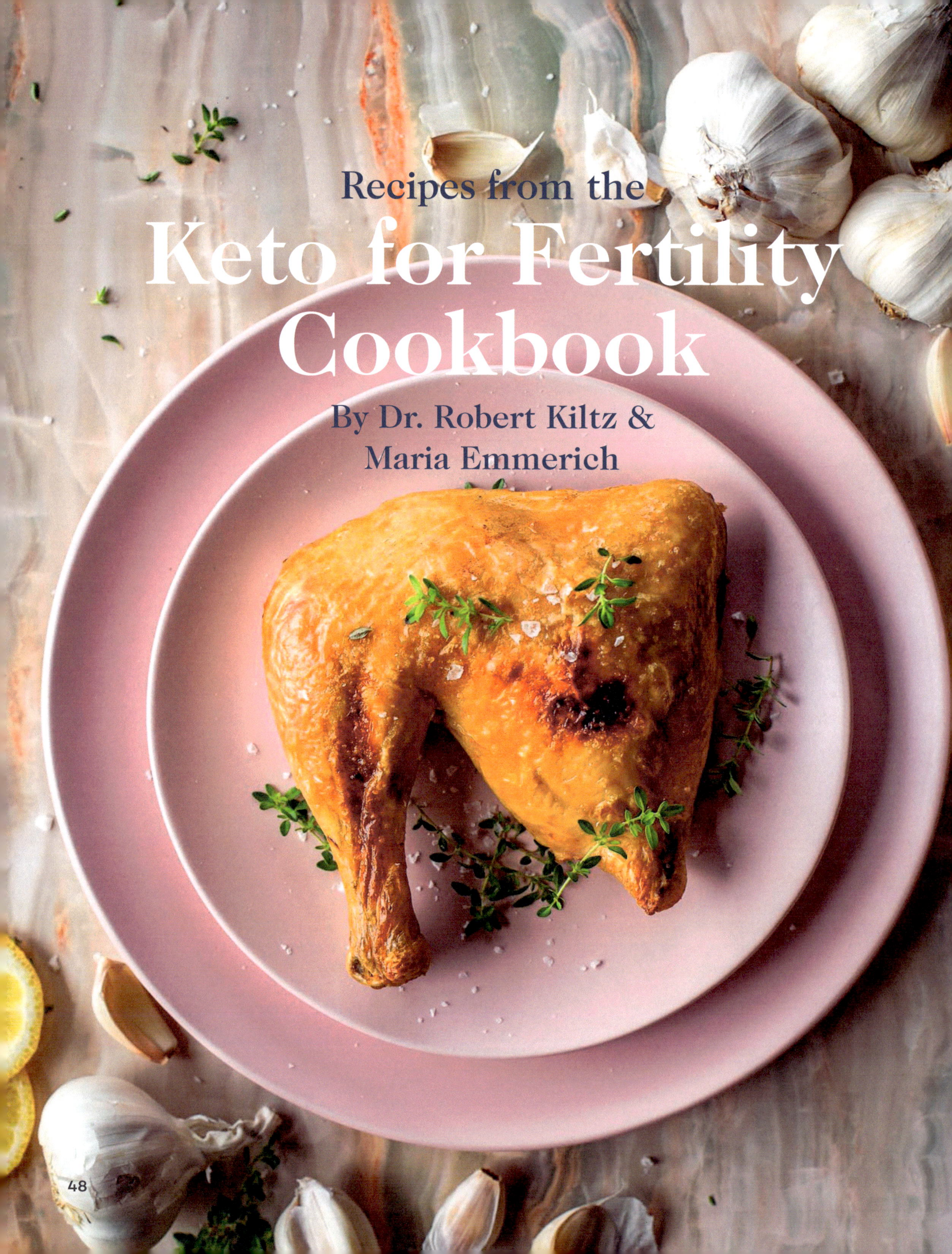

Recipes from the

Keto for Fertility Cookbook

By Dr. Robert Kiltz & Maria Emmerich

NUTRITIONAL INFORMATION

Calories: 379
Fat: 30g
Protein: 23g
Carbs: 2g
Fiber: 0.5g

Easy Chicken Confit

Prep: 7 minutes
Cook: 45 minutes
Yield: 4 servings

INGREDIENTS

- 4 bone-in skin on, chicken thighs
- 2 teaspoons Redmond Real salt
- ¼ cup diced onion
- 3 cloves garlic, minced
- 4 springs fresh thyme
- 1 lemon, sliced
- 1 cup melted duck fat or olive oil

INSTRUCTIONS

1. Preheat oven to 325 degrees F.
2. Season the chicken with salt. Place them in a baking dish so they fit snuggly in one layer. Top with onions, garlic, thyme and slices of lemon. Cover with melted duck fat or olive oil.
3. Bake for 45-55 minutes or until chicken is cooked through and no longer pink inside. Discard excess oil from the dish.
4. Turn oven to broil and place the chicken in the oven with skin side up for 3 to 5 minutes or until skin is crispy. Best served fresh.

NUTRITIONAL INFORMATION

Calories: 571
Fat: 47g
Protein: 34g
Carbs: 1g
Fiber: 0.3g

Seared Porterhouse

Prep: 6 minutes
Cook: 8 minutes
Yield: 2 servings

INGREDIENTS

- 1 (16-ounce) **porterhouse steak**, about 1 inch thick
- 1 teaspoon fine sea salt
- ½ teaspoon fresh ground black pepper
- 1 tablespoon duck fat
- 3 tablespoons unsalted butter
- 1 tablespoon fresh thyme or tarragon leaves.

INSTRUCTIONS

1. Remove the steak from the fridge about 20 minutes before you plan to cook it. Pat it dry and season with the salt and pepper.
2. Place the duck fat in large skillet over medium-high heat. Once hot, **sear the steak for 2 minutes,** without moving it, then flip it over and sear it for another 2 minutes.
3. Lower the heat to medium-low and add the butter and herbs. Using a spoon, constantly pour the "liquid gold" (aka butter) over the steak. **Continue to baste and cook the steak for about 4 more minutes per side for medium-rare.** The exact timing will depend on how thick your steak is.
4. Once cooked to your desired doneness, remove the steak from the pan and **allow to rest at room temperature for 5 minutes before cutting** to make sure that the juices stay in the steak. Pour the butter into a small serving dish for dipping the steak. Best served fresh.

NUTRITIONAL INFORMATION

Calories: 379
Fat: 30g
Protein: 23g
Carbs: 2g
Fiber: 0.5g

Bacon Ice Cream Cones

Prep: 5 minutes
Cook: 15 minutes
Yield: 12 servings

INGREDIENTS

- 12 slices thick cut bacon.

INSTRUCTIONS

1. Preheat oven to 400°F.
2. Line a large baking sheet with defined edges with unbleached parchment paper.
3. Using cone-shaped metal (we made our own with sheet metal), wrap one slice of bacon around each. Wrap the bacon tightly, overlapping the edges so the bacon totally covers the cone.
4. Bake for 15-20 minutes or until bacon is crisp. Remove from oven and allow to totally cool.
5. Meanwhile make Kiltz's Keto Ice Cream (see recipe on page 112)

NUTRITIONAL INFORMATION

Calories: 283g
Fat: 17.5g
Protein: 27.5g
Carbs: 1.6g
Fiber: 0g

Beefy Breakfast Muffins

Prep: 7 minutes
Cook: 32 minutes
Yield: 6 servings

INGREDIENTS

- 1 pound ground beef
- ¼ pound ground liver (or more ground beef)
- 1 ¼ teaspoon Redmond Real salt
- 6 small eggs
- 4 slices bacon, cut into thirds crosswise

INSTRUCTIONS

1. **Preheat oven to 375 degrees F**. Grease a large 6-well muffin tin (or 6 large ramekins) and set aside.
2. Place the ground beef, ground liver into a medium bowl. Season with salt and combine well with your hands.
3. Divide the meat mixture between the muffin tin (or ramekins)
4. Use your thumbs to create a large enough well in each meat muffin so that it can hold an entire egg. Crack one egg into each well of the meat muffin.
5. Top each egg with 2 pieces of the bacon, making an "x."
6. **Place in the oven and bake for 30 minutes.** Turn the oven to broil and continue cooking for 2 minutes to crisp the bacon.
7. Remove from oven and allow to cool for about 10 minutes before removing from the muffin tin. Feel free to eat right out of the ramekins.
8. Store extras in an airtight container in the fridge for up to 4 days. To reheat, place in a 350 degree F oven for 3 minutes or until heated through. Then increase oven to broil for 1 minute to crisp the bacon.

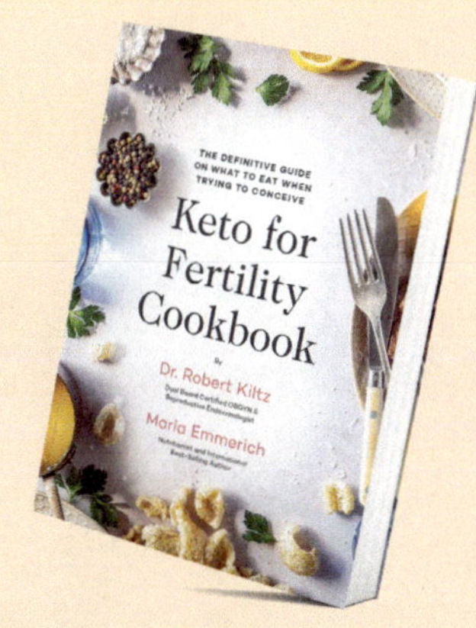

Keto for Fertility Cookbook

Want more recipes and information about how and why a HFLC food plan works scientifically to improve your fertility?

Keto for Fertility Cookbook is available for sale at https://ketoforfertility.co/

Dining Out on Carnivore

Many people do well sticking to carnivore when they are preparing meals themselves. It's another story entirely when traveling for work or meeting friends for dinner at a restaurant.

Between the bread basket in the center of the table and a long list of tempting (but not carnivore-friendly) appetizers to share, it can be a struggle to stick with the plan. The good news is that as carnivore eating has become more popular, many restaurants have adapted their menus.

DINING TIPS:

- If you have a say about where you'll be eating, your best bet is a steak house, seafood restaurant, Greek or Middle Eastern restaurant, or Chinese. Some BBQ places can work as well. Try to steer clear of pizza joints and smaller Mexican or Italian restaurants which may be limited to carb-heavy options.
- **Take a look at the menu in advance.** Most restaurants post their menus online so you can review your options without stress.
- **Don't be afraid to ask questions.** You may need to ask how something is cooked or prepared to find out if it's really a good choice.
- **Avoid dressings and sauces** or ask for them on the side. They contain lots of hidden sugar.
- **Grab a snack beforehand** so you're not starving once you get to the restaurant—a fat bomb or some chunks of parmesan cheese. The basket of bread is a whole lot more tempting when your stomach is grumbling.

WHAT TO ORDER

- Burger without a bun (but skip the fries)
- Chicken wings (most restaurants have these on the appetizer menu)
- Meat, chicken, or fatty fish that isn't breaded or fried. Ask for a side of butter to help add the fat
- When all else fails, a cup of coffee with heavy cream is a readily available on-the-go filler until you find a better option

Alcohol: Many people like to share a bottle of wine or grab a beer over dinner. I generally warn against alcohol. It's toxic and fuels inflammation in the gut. Most wines and mixed drinks have lots of sugar (and phytochemicals). And there's a reason we don't allow kids to drink. But even I, from time to time, have something alcoholic to drink while socializing. When I do, it's a very dirty martini with a couple blue cheese stuffed olives.

Remember: If you have a bite of dessert or steal a fry from a friend's plate, it's not the end of the world and certainly not worth beating yourself up over. Do the best you can to make smart choices and move on from there.

Many restaurants have adapted their menus and even note carnivore and keto-friendly options.

Kiltz's Carnivore is for Life

SUSTAINABILITY

Patients and friends ask me all the time whether carnivore is a sustainable way of life. People are so convinced they cannot live without sugar, bread, and various fruits and vegetables that they refuse to accept any reality where those things aren't required.

You can absolutely live without sugar or bread. I eat sweet stuff (Kiltz's Ice Cream) and occasionally French fries dipped in mayo. But. I don't need it, and it's not really necessary. But I too enjoy it from time to time

Dr. Kiltz's Carnivore Lifestyle is simple: **Eat less and less frequently.** More fasting equals more lasting! Eat one meal and one to two snacks a day and get more rest. We all love variety and spice, yet this turns out to be unhealthy for the human animal. We can enjoy the fruits of life from time to time, but not all the time.

The carnivore concept is sustainable. It is what we are built for. **Fuel the body with the life sustaining energy it needs – FAT.**

All plants primarily breakdown to simple sugars, which must be converted to fat in the liver. All of those healthy fruits and vegetables breakdown to simple unhealthy sugars in the G.I. tract. Yet they are not in and of themselves unhealthy. But simply eating them all the time makes them poison.**The dose/frequency/duration makes the poison.**

Only you can determine what is sustainable emotionally or physically. **Carnivore is for me. It's healthy. It's easy. It's simple.** I know people like Maria Emmerich who have lived keto for the majority of their lives, raised their kids on it and now it's carnivore as a family. She has cook book after cook book with recipes that are flavorful and satisfying. It's a change in mindset for sure, but the results are undeniable.

People have the impression that being a vegetarian or vegan is so healthy. I'm not knocking the decision to be either, but the reality is that neither of these lifestyles would work without grocery stores to provide enough food and calories to satisfy your nutritional needs. Animal fat and protein is a lot more efficient and satiating then any leaf, flower, seed or nut.

DR. KILTZ'S CARNIVORE LIFESTYLE HAS 1 MEAL / 1-2 SNACKS / 1 NAP/ INFINITE MINDFUL MOMENTS PER DAY.

"Be open to something you do not believe. Listen and learn. Be a receptive vessel."

-Robert Kiltz

The Adjustment Phase

Change is difficult. Physically, mentally, and emotionally. Starting a carnivore lifestyle is no different. You're eating fewer calories (sometimes), on a different schedule, and from mainly animal sources. It takes time for your body to adjust to fewer carbs and chemicals. **Here are some temporary side effects you may experience along the way.**

Adaptation Symptoms

Headaches or Migraines

Brain Fog

Lack of Energy and General Fatigue (mental and physical)

Dizziness or balance issues

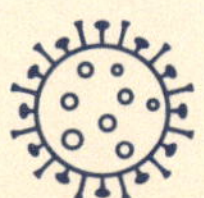

Flu-like symptoms

Muscle Aches

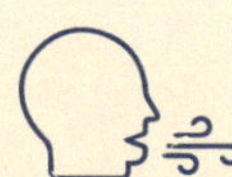

Bad breath or metallic taste in your mouth

Sore Throat

Nausea

Diarrhea

Difficulty sleeping

Night Sweats

Reducing Adaptation Symptoms:

DRINK ENOUGH WATER & ELECTROLYTES:
Make sure you increase your water consumption and add in electrolytes (sodium, potassium, magnesium, and chloride) to make up for what you are losing in water weight. Staying hydrated can help alleviate symptoms like muscle cramps and fatigue.

GET ADEQUATE SLEEP:
Insomnia and interrupted sleep are both common symptoms during the transition phase. Sometimes restricting water consumption just before bed and not eating during the 3-4 hours before bedtime may help prevent nighttime bathroom visits. Optimize sleep conditions by making sure your room is cool and dark, taking a bath or shower to relax, and establish a consistent schedule that you stick to 7 days a week.

EAT FATTY MEAT TO SATIATION:
Stay full and don't restrict how much or how often you eat. Don't count calories. Fat is your purest energy source, and eating enough of it can reduce cravings you keep you feeling satisfied. Also, slowly cutting back on carbs and increasing your fat intake can decrease symptoms as you transition.

BREAK A SWEAT:
Sweating is our body's natural way of detoxifying. Sweating during some light to moderate exercise can help you sleep better and cleanse the body of toxins, but avoid strenuous exercise while your experiencing adaptation symptoms.

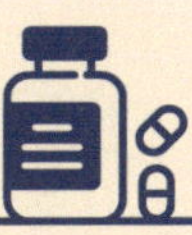

CONSIDER SUPPLEMENTS:
Lipase supplements can help G.I. unrest as your body acclimates to higher fat intake. Ox Bile can also be added if Lipase doesn't appear to ease your symptoms.

"If exercise were a drug, it would be the best drug we have for preventing heart disease. But like with any drug, you've got to get the dose right."

—Dr. James O'Keefe, Cardiologist

Survival of the ~~Fittest~~ Moderately Fit

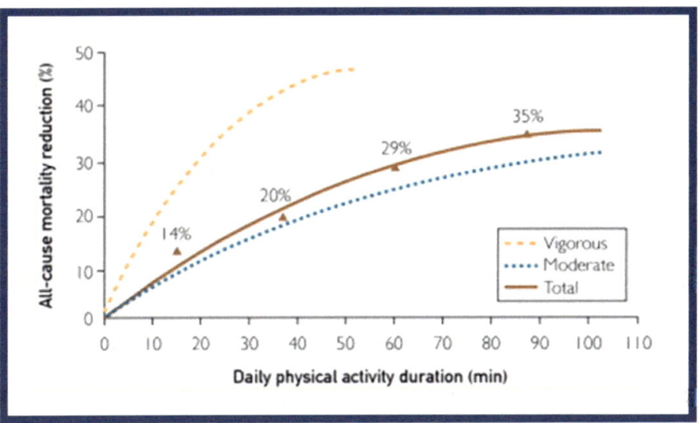

The mortality benefits of exercise appear with even smaller amounts of daily exercise and peak at 50 to 60 minutes of vigorous exercise per day.

LIGHT WEIGHTS, WALKING, YOGA . . . THAT'S THE SWEET SPOT.

If a little bit is good, a lot must be great, right? When it comes to exercise (and a lot of other things too), this couldn't be further from the truth. Cardiologist Dr. James O'Keefe investigated the impact of excessive endurance exercise on cardiovascular health. He found that, just like a prescription drug, there's an ideal "dose" of exercise, and it's light to moderate.

Marathoners/extreme endurance athletes could be shortening their life expectancy because these types of activities require sustained increases in cardiac output and stress that can damage the heart and large arteries as a result of repeated cycles of damage.

After a marathon, you'll find elevated levels of troponin in about half of participants. This is chemical that is released when heart muscle dies and a heart attack is imminent. In marathoners, these are little micro-tears in the heart from the stretching and exertion that will heal quickly with no longer term effects. But this type of exertion over and over can create scars, thickening, and other structural changes to the heart chambers.

Most long-term studies show a recurring pattern of reverse-J or U-curves whereby light to moderate doses of physical activity, such as walking or jogging, reduce premature death rates by 30% to 50%; however, partial or complete loss of these benefits are noted with chronic very high doses of exercise.

BOTTOM LINE

A lack of physical activity is an even bigger threat to your cardiac health. If you are exercising to improve your long-term cardiovascular health and longevity, aim for moderate instead of extreme efforts, and be sure to take at least one day per week off of strenuous exercise.

Stick to light to moderate forms of exercise—walking, jogging, leisurely bicycling, gardening, yoga, resistance work, etc. Even sex can be a healthy form of exercise.

Cream is The New Orange Juice

Adding **full-fat heavy cream or butter** to your coffee or tea is an easy way to add fat back in to your diet, and it tastes great too! Give up the non-dairy creamers, sugary flavored mix-ins, almond or soy milk. Go with full-fat heavy cream to fight inflammation.

Find the Fat

MAKE BACON, EGGS, BUTTER, BEEF & SALT THE MAINSTAYS OF YOUR REGULAR DIET

Anyone who has spoken to me has heard me repeat these five foods like a mantra. They are the basis of Dr. Kiltz's B.E.B.B.I.S. Diet. **They point back to this simple truth: Our bodies require fat for energy. If we can't eat fat or make fat, we die.** Unfortunately, the majority of fat we consume is industrial, man-made fat. What we really need to be eating is nature's fat—that stuff that surrounds the animal or is intertwined and marbled in every nook and cranny of the meat.

Stay away from lean meats and try to choose grass-fed, all-natural meats. You want to consume fatty meats like a rib-eye steak, not lean, fat-free chicken breast. You need to eat the fat. By adding fat, cream, butter, and eggs, you reduce inflammation, you reduce your appetite, you reduce your glucose levels, and your energy is so much better. All of the bowel problems go away, the skin problems and the joint problems are gone.

Minimize the variety and simplify your meals. Eliminate pasta, bread, yogurt, milk, seeds, and nuts. Plant oils which harden when exposed to oxygen likely contain a multitude of plant antigens, which are harmful.

Eating fat in its purest form is the simplest energy source for our bodies. There are a lot of different food plans out there that focus on high fat / med-low protein / low carbs. They are pretty similar, but tend to differentiate themselves by their recommended fat and carb consumption. Paleo is about 20% protein, 70% fat, 10% carbs. **The B.E.B.B.I.S. Diet is 80% fat, 20% protein, zero carbs.** This is the key to health and wellness.Any combination of bacon, eggs, butter, and beef (or fatty meat) is crucial to reducing inflammation. We call this ***The Lion King Plan.*** To eat like the king of the jungle means eliminating all fruits and vegetables that produce sugar and phytochemicals, and focusing only on high quality, high fat foods.

THINGS TO AVOID:

- Sugar
- Carbohydrates
- Alcohol
- High-intensity exercise
- Probiotics
- Fiber
- Seeds & nuts

Good Animal Fats vs. Bad Plant Fats

It goes without saying, but not all fats are created equal. We see lots of lists of "Good Fats" and "Bad Fats" but even those labels are misleading. And can fat really come from a vegetable? Not without a lot of help from humans to extract it. Any oil that isn't solid at room temperature should be avoided, in my opinion. Vegetable oils are extracted from seeds and nuts which carry a host of harmful plant antigens and phytochemicals. So, while we might think of them as "heart healthy", they are certainly not immune-friendly.

ALL PLANT BASED OILS = INDUSTRIAL PRODUCTS

Oil Type	PUFA	SFA
Coconut Oil	1.9%	92.0%
Palm Oil	2.0%	82.0%
Cocoa Butter	3.0%	60.0%
Beef Tallow	3.1%	49.8%
Ghee	4.0%	48.0%
Butter	3.4%	50.0%
High Oleic Sunflower Oil	9.0%	
Macadamia Oil	10.0%	15.0%
Avocado Oil	10.0%	11.0%
Lard	12.0%	41.0%
Duck Fat	13.0%	25.0%
Hazelnut Oil	14.0%	10.0%
Almond Oil	17.0%	8.20%
Olive Oil	9.90%	14.0%

Source: mariamindbodyhealth.com

*Don't use olive oil for cooking. Heating it will cause oxidation. Only use in dressings.

To help protect against heart disease, you want to increase your intake of fat, particularly saturated fatty acids (SFAs). Fat in its best and purest, most natural form comes from animals (lard, tallow, butter, ghee, duck fat). Secondarily, there are several fruits and vegetables that are high in fat, like coconut oil, cocoa butter, and hemp seed oil. They protect against oxidation and inflammation and have many other important health benefits.

Stay away from vegetable oils like soybean, canola, vegetable, sunflower, and corn oil. They lower your good LDL. The higher the saturated fat content, the better:

FATS TO AVOID

Good fats come from animals, Bad "fats" come from plants = oils.

All plant oils are industrial oils that are not good for us. Animal fats are much healthier. If you choose to use plant oils, I recommend coconut oil.

Super Foods Have Us Super Fooled, NOT Super Fueled

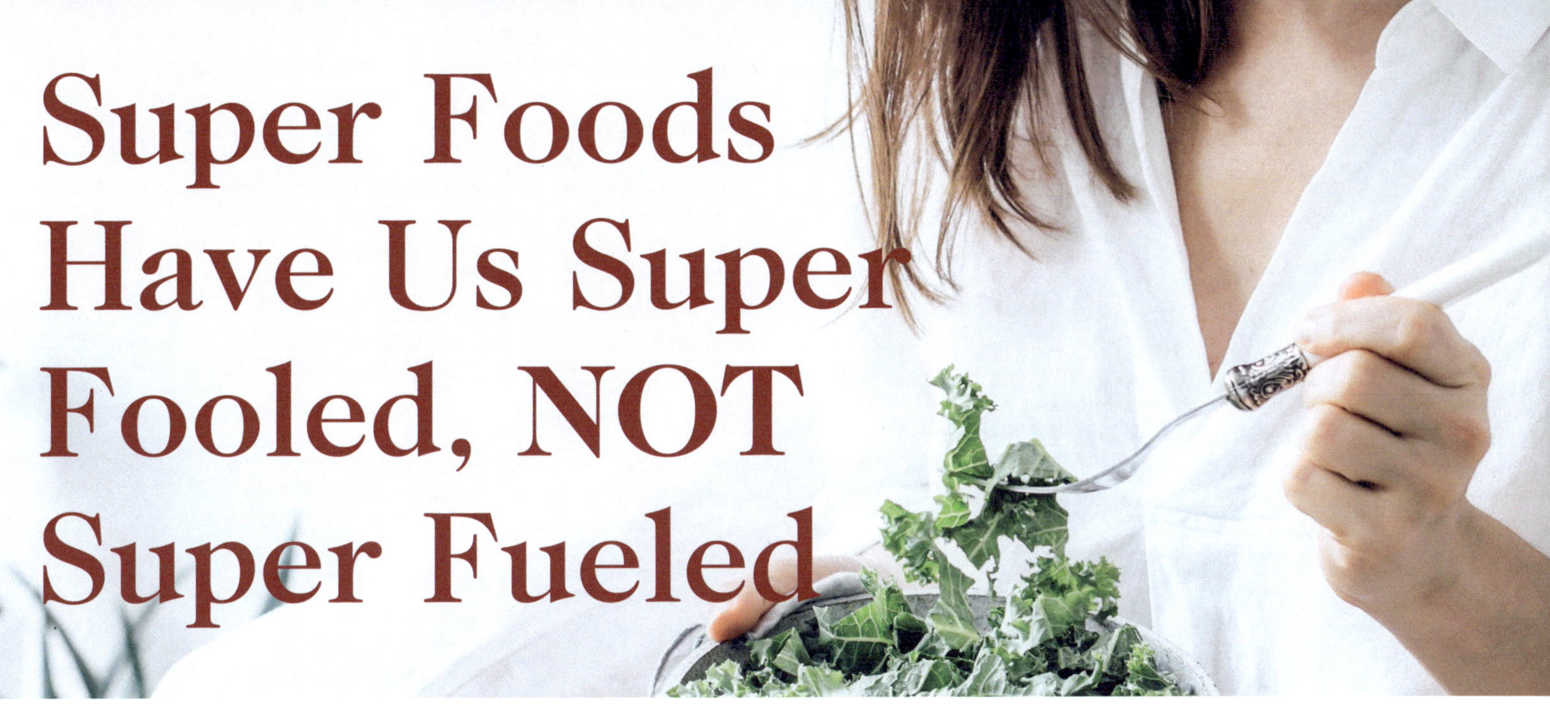

NUTRIENTS IN SUPERFOODS COMPARED TO ANIMAL PROTEIN

Per Serving	Apples	Blueberries	Kale	Beef	Beef Liver
Calcium (mg)	9.1	4.5	63.4	11	11
Magnesium (mg)	7.3	4.5	15.0	19	18
Phosphorus (mg)	20.0	9.0	24.6	175	387
Potassium (mg)	163.8	57.8	200.6	370	380
Iron (mg)	0.2	0.2	0.8	3.3	8.8
Zinc (mg)	0.2	0.2	0.2	4.5	4
Selenium (mcg)	0.0	0.1	0.4	14.2	39.7
Vitamin A (IU)	69.2	40.5	13530.9	40	53,400
Vitamin B6 (mg)	0.0	0.1	0.1	0.4	1.1
Vitamin B12 (mcg)	0.0	0.0	0.0	2	11
Vitamin C (mg)	7.3	7.3	36.1	2	27
Vitamin D (IU)	0.0	0.0	0.0	7	19
Vitamin E (mg)	0.2	0.5	0.8	1.7	0.63
Niacin (mg)	0.2	0.3	0.4	4.8	17
Folate (mcg)	0.0	4.5	11.4	6	145

Chart Source: *Keto: The Complete Guide to Success on The Ketogenic Diet, including Simplified Science and No-cook Meal Plans.*

There are lots of health food buzz words out there: antioxidants, super foods, multi-grain, GMO-free, artisanal, organic, all-natural, pro-biotic, but what do they really mean? We are told they pack a nutritional wallop, and we should pack them in our carts every chance we get. A year or two ago, everything was KALE. Kale chips, kale salads, kale smoothies. And before that, it was blueberries.

They sure sound good, but do they really do everything we're told they do? If they did, I think we'd all be a whole lot healthier and taking fewer prescription drugs. If you asked 50 people to answer "What's healthy for us?", you would likely get 50 different answers, but the majority of them would be greatly influenced by food marketing and advertising. We believe the hype and believe what we read on the packaging and hear in commercials.

There is nothing that comes in a box or a bag that is any better for our bodies than animal fat and protein. And to carnivore naysayers who think meat cannot provide all of the vitamins found in fruits and vegetables . . . think again!

The Incredible Egg

WHY EGGS ARE THE PERFECT CARNIVORE FOOD

Egg yolks got a bad rap for quite a while. Health conscious consumers ditched them and put egg white omelets on breakfast tables and in restaurants around the country. While egg whites are a great source of protein, if you're just eating the white, you're missing out. Here's why: egg yolks contain other essential nutrients like Vitamin A, D, E, K, B12, folate, choline and even the beneficial antioxidant lutein. Eggs are the perfect blend of low carb, high fat, high protein, and they are so versatile. Fried, scrambled, hard boiled, soft boiled, poached, in egg salad, omelets, and frittatas. Breakfast, lunch, and dinner, eggs provide the nutrients you need in a perfect little package that's super affordable too. A large egg contains less than 1 gram of carbs, 5 grams of fat, and approximately 6 grams of protein—ideal for keto.

You could say that eggs are the new apples . . . an egg a day will keep the doctor away and with none of the sugar!

NUTRIONAL VALUES COMPARISON CHART (100g each)- Egg with vegetables

Nutrients	Egg	Potato	Spinach	Cauliflower	Green Peas	Tomato	Brinjal
Choline (mg)	294	12.1	19.3	44.3	28.4	6.7	6.9
Iron (mg)	1.75	0.78	2.71	0.42	1.47	0.27	0.24
E.A.A (gm)	5.6	0.6	1.11	0.75	1.4	0.17	0.33
Protein (gm)	12.6	2	2.86	1.92	5.4	0.88	1
Folic Acid (mcg)	47	16	194	57	65	15	22
Zn (mg)	1.29	0.29	0.53	0.27	1.24	0.17	0.16
Calories (Kcal)	63	77	23	25	83	18	24
Vit. A (IU)	540	2	9377	absent	765	833	27
Vit. E (mg)	1.05	0.01	2.03	0.08	0.13	0.54	0.3
Phosporus (mg)	198	57	49	44	108	24	25
Good Fat (gm)	5.6	0.045	0.175	0.017	0.22	0.114	0.092
Calcium (mg)	56	12	22	22	25	10	9

"An ***egg a day*** *will keep the doctor away –with none of the sugar!"*

The Dangers of Complex & Simple Carbohydrates

IF WHAT YOU'RE EATING ISN'T EITHER FAT OR A PROTEIN, IT'S SUGAR.

The average American consumes a staggering 3 pounds of sugar each week, much of it "hidden" in processed foods, sauces, and drinks. Worldwide, most of us eat 500 extra calories a day just from sugar. It's quite common for food manufacturers to bump up the sugar for flavor when they make a product low-fat. And that fancy drink from the coffee shop or dressing on the "healthy" salad you had for lunch has a lot more sugar than you would guess.

When people hear the word "sugar", they visualize the white granular stuff used in baking cakes. **This type of sugar can be deadly if consumed too often, but even more dangerous are the leafy greens, fruits, and vegetables.** They too are sugar, but they come with the added danger of plant antigens and phytochemicals, bacteria, yeast, and viruses. To this end, seeds and nuts are also harmful to your body despite what you may have heard.

Do we need to eat carbs? In a word, NO. We do not need to eat carbs. Ever. Just like your liver makes fat and cholesterol, it also makes **glucose,** which can be broken down and used for energy by every cell in the body.

Your liver can make all the glucose it needs from just about anything—protein, fat, or carbs. Contrary to what you might hear and think, sugar is a non-essential part of our diet. Sugar is a quick energy source and breaks down quickly, but fat is a much better fuel.

Sugar goes by over 60 different names: glucose, fructose, sucrose, maltose, just to name a few, but our body can't tell the difference between them, and they are all processed the same—sent to the liver to be converted into fat. Although we're told that lettuce, for example, is a "complex" carb, it's really full of **glucose** because all plant material we consume is sugar. Our body processes lettuce the same as it would mostly sugar.

HERE ARE SOME THINGS I'VE LEARNED ABOUT SUGAR:

Sugar is addictive. If you've ever felt like you might have a sugar addiction, you are likely closer to the truth than you imagined. When you eat sugar, you activate opiate and dopamine receptors in your brain. Ironically, these are the same "happy" chemicals that cause you to feel good when hanging out with loved ones and good friends. But with sugar, we get stuck in a compulsive loop of consumption despite the negative consequences like weight gain, hormone imbalances, and inflammation. Studies suggest that every time we eat sweets, we are reinforcing those neuropathways, causing the brain to become increasingly hardwired to crave sugar. The more sugar we eat, the more tolerance we build up, as with any other drug. Furthermore, the drive to eat carbs/sugar is built into our DNA for survival. It's seasonally available and gets us fat so that we are able to survive for the next weeks and months until we can find food.

Sugar hides in many non-sugary foods. As I mentioned earlier, sugar is an ingredient in most packaged and processed foods even when they are not necessarily what we think of as sweet. Ketchup, salad dressings, marinades, jarred tomato sauce, granola bars, yogurt, BBQ sauce, sports drinks, canned soups, cereal, breads, smoothies and even protein shakes are some great examples of grocery items with hidden sugar. Take a look at the nutrition label on your favorite snack or condiment. You might be surprised! It's not enough to just avoid cookies, cakes, pastries, and the obvious suspects. This is one of the reasons I feel so strongly that people should avoid buying and eating anything processed and/or packaged. Natural is best, and mostly prepare it yourself or know and trust who is, so you know exactly what you're eating.

Excessive sugar has the same toxic effect . . . on the liver as alcohol. There are lots of people who strongly feel that sugar should get the same type of warnings we see on alcohol. Why? Because there's evidence that fructose and glucose in excess quantities can have the same toxic effect on the liver as alcohol. Sugar also increases the risk for several of the same chronic conditions that alcohol causes. And being a healthy weight doesn't make you immune from liver damage caused by fructose. Studies show that liver damage can occur even without excess calories or weight gain.

Sugar may be aging your brain. All of that excess sugar you are eating is likely accelerating the aging process. Scientists have discovered a positive relationship between **glucose** consumption and the aging of our cells. Aging cells can result in something as minor as wrinkles and as concerning as chronic disease. Excessive sugar consumption has also been linked to deficiencies in memory and overall cognitive health. Excess **glucose** in our bowels and blood vessels are distributed to every cell and organ in our bodies, which causes damage via glycation. **Glucose** in excess amounts damages the glycocalyx (the Teflon coating of every cellular-epithelial lining of our body that is there to protect us from damage). This damage creates inflammation, which leads to all disease.

Sugar and carbs are making us fat. Fat is not making us fat. Because of its lack of nutrients, sugar makes it easy to consume lots of it and not fully understand the dangers. With no immediate negative physical effects to warn us of the perils, we keep on eating it. Fats and proteins offer a sense of fullness and satiation. Sugar gives you calories, but not the full feeling that you've had enough you get when you eat fat or protein. That's why you can eat an entire bag of candy at the movies and still be ready for dinner after the credits roll.

That fruits and vegetables are in fact sugar makes the recommendations by the American Diabetes Association and the American Heart Association so unscientific to me. I lost my beautiful sister, Maria Ann, to diabetes. She was diagnosed at age four. She died at 52 from heart disease and blindness as a result of diabetes. I now know that the diet recommended to her by the nutritional and medical experts was completely wrong.

Sugar comes from all plant material. Eating a diet rich in fresh fruits and vegetables, as they recommend, raises **glucose** levels in the body. In a diabetic, this expedites organ damage.

Yet, alas, famines are rare to most of us in the western world. Sweet is sweet and addictive for a reason. When available, we must eat it, since it will rot soon. Then it is gone, and we will have missed our opportunity to consumer an important source for creating fat.

Fat is our cellular energy always! We must convert sugar/proteins/simple sugars/amino acids to fat in our liver or we die. The live is critical for producing fat via the insulin dependent reactions and pathways. Simple sugars and amino acids are transported to the liver, converted to fat, then stored in the liver, and transported to all part of the body, providing the only fuel for every cell: Acetyl CoA from the lightspeed conversion from fat (triglycerides).

SUGARS - FEED THE BACTERIA & THE YEAST TO FERMENT & MAKE ALCOHOL

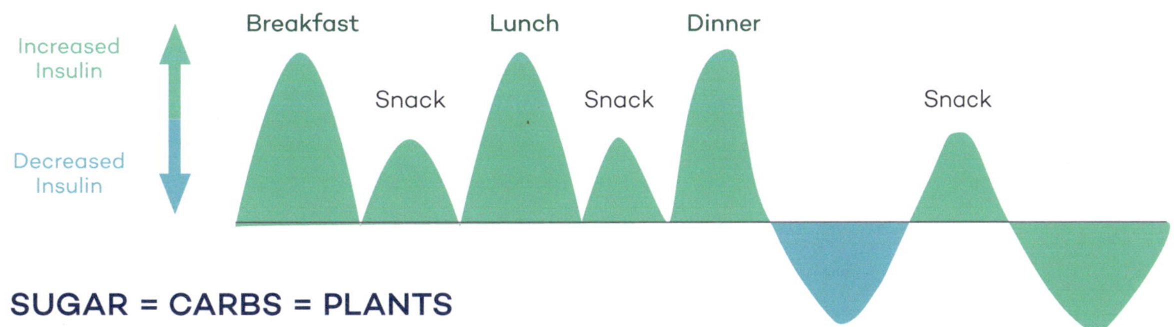

How Can Fruits & Vegetables Be Bad for Us?

Vegetables are sugar. Whole grains (which come from plants) are sugar too. This is a simple yet difficult truth for many to accept. Other than the revelation that fat is actually good for us, the one component of Dr. Kiltz's Carnivore that is particularly surprising to anyone I talk to is the fact that I recommend little to no fruits, vegetables, and fiber to be consumed. For those who grew up with the idea that a big salad was the epitome of health, this is a direct challenge to all they know.

Fruits and vegetables are carbohydrates, and many of them contain high amounts of sugar (just check out the glycemic index on some of the more common fruits and vegetables you likely eat). They also contain a tremendous number of plant antigens and phytochemicals that can be dangerous and even deadly to our bodies. Phytochemicals are molecules that actually harm our bodies on a cellular level.

While our ancestors did eat some fruits and vegetables while they were ripe and in season (likely during summer months), the basis of their diet was animal meat. What's more, the fruits and veggies they did eat look **NOTHING** like what we're buying year-round from the produce section of our grocery stores. Scientists have hybridized and cultivated most produce to be bigger, sweeter, juicier, and available 365 days a year.

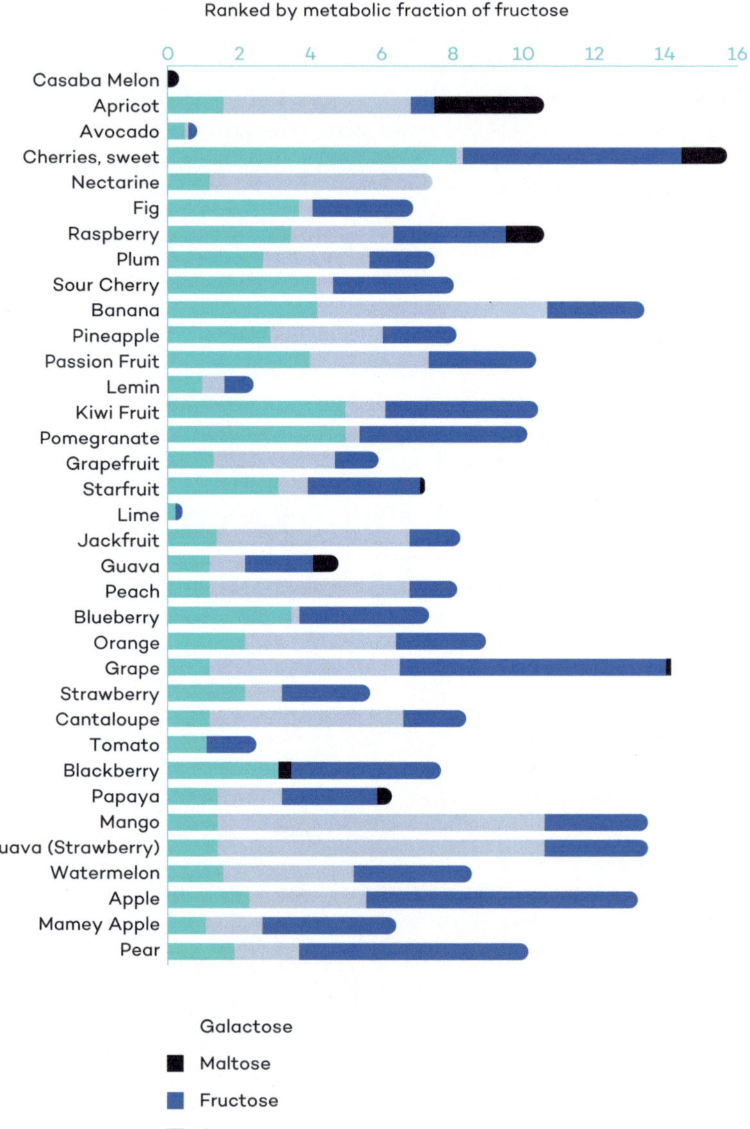

Plant Problems

√ Sugar

√ Bacteria

√ Lectins

√ Cyanide

√ Toxins (e.g. phytates,tannins, oxalates)

√ Hormone Disruptors

√ Nutrient Blockers

√ Photo Sensitivity

√ Night Shades

We humans eat every part of the plant, from seeds to roots, stems, leaves, and fruit. We eat it all! Whether it's in the form of chocolate chip cookies or that bowl of oatmeal with brown sugar and raisins, we are all consuming a high-plant-based diet. Oats are the seeds of a plant. Sugar comes from a plant. Raisins are fruit. Most of our "unhealthy" foods are simply derived from our "healthy" plant-based foods consumed in excessive amount and frequency.

Why is that dangerous you might ask? Well, plants are very clever. Much like animals, they too are built for survival. Most plants don't have the benefit of sharp teeth or talons to protect their leaves. While some may have thorns, frequently their tools of survival are invisible to humans and other predators. They're hidden and take the form of phytochemicals and antigens. Most plants pose no threat until they are ingested.

Lectins are one of the ways plants protect themselves and their seeds. Lectins are a protein produced by plants as a natural insecticide. Humans have even genetically engineered some plants to produce extra lectins to ward off insects. Unfortunately, humans aren't immune to their damaging effect.

We can't digest many lectins, so some get into our G.I. tract completely intact where they can inflict damage by chelating the important minerals and vitamins, preventing their ingestion, and allowing bacteria, yeast, and viruses into our blood stream, creating an immune response that is inflammation. Plant antigens have the ability to disrupt communication between cells when one neuron is trying to relay a message to another neuron. This includes disrupting endocrine receptors and hormone function.

A lectin-free diet would basically eliminate all plant-based foods. In this light, it's not surprising that the Carnivore Diet is so effective at reducing inflammation.

"Most of our "unhealthy" foods are simply derived from our "healthy" plant-based foods."

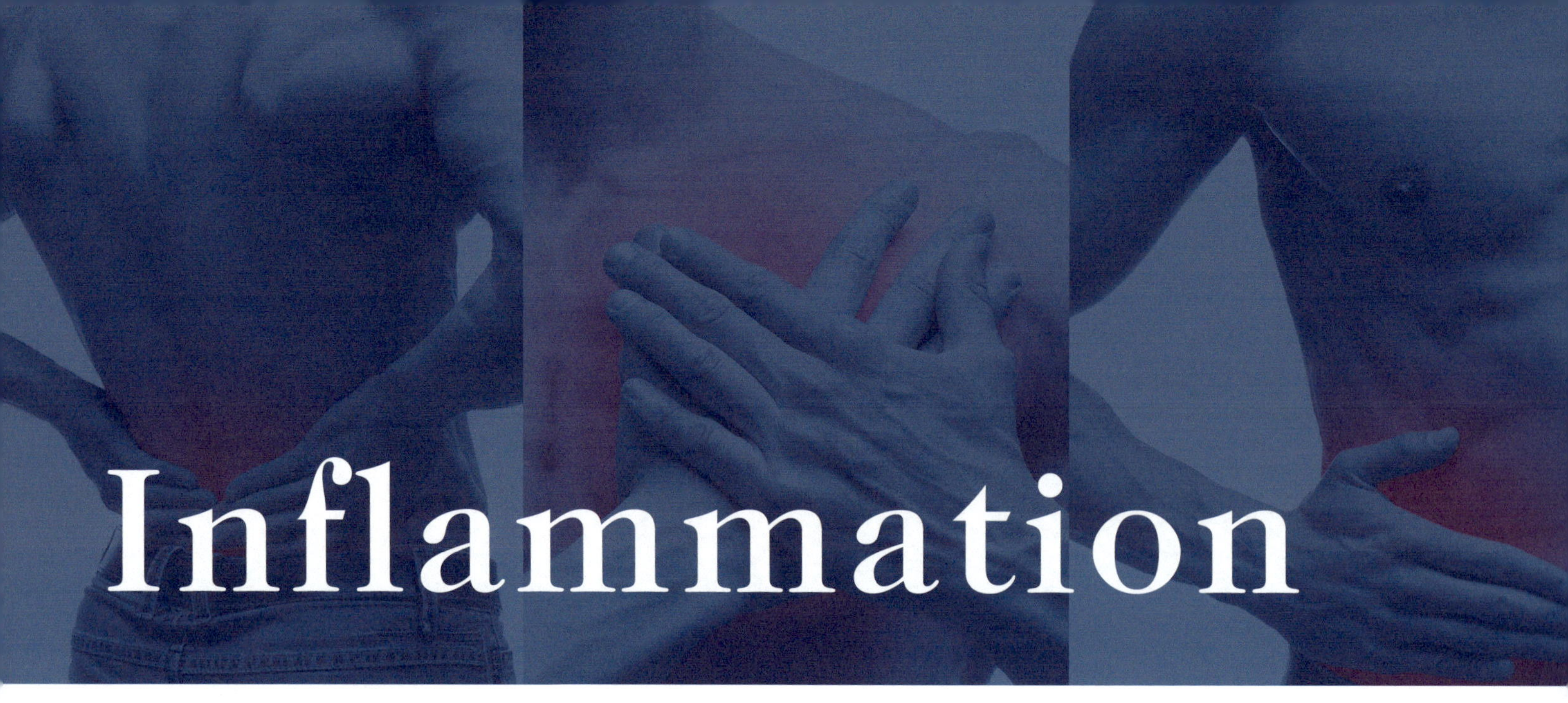

Inflammation

THE CAUSE OF ALL DISEASE

In order to understand **Dr. Kiltz's Carnivore Lifestyle** and why it works, you first must understand inflammation, what are its likely causes, and the havoc it wreaks on every cell, organ and system in our bodies.

The body's immune response is a mysterious thing. When it functions properly, inflammation is a quick response that actually helps the body to heal. But when it doesn't turn off, inflammation simmers at a chronic level and begins to damage healthy cells instead of healing damaged cells, contributing to a long list of diseases. A systemic acute anaphylactic inflammation can kill quickly.

Cardinal signs of inflammation include swelling, redness, heat, pain, and ultimately dysfunction that can result in cellular failure and even organ failure. But Inflammation isn't always obvious. It can appear as joint pain or swelling, as well as gum disease, fatigue, headaches, unexplained rashes, and muscle stiffness. Sometimes inflammation goes unnoticed until a diagnosis of heart disease, diabetes, or an autoimmune condition (where the immune system mistakenly attacks your body) such as lupus, multiple sclerosis, and rheumatoid arthritis.

Inflammation is linked to nearly all of our diseases. Infertility is just one among a long list of diseases caused by acute and chronic inflammation due to infection from a microorganism, or glucose and glycation, or various phytochemicals and plant antigens—lectins and particles of plant material that actually elicit inflammatory responses from our own body.

Why exactly it happens in the uterus, tubes, ovaries or in the male reproductive organs, we're not completely sure, but I believe it has to do with the blood flow that deposits these microorganisms and plant phytochemicals and antigens in those areas. Plus, it's secondary to the excessive heat in the G.I. tract—the colon and small intestines—and as the fermentation of these particles (fruits, fibers, vegetables) occurs, it creates an exothermic reaction that heats and damages the local organs and tissues.

Inflammation is the body's reaction to these insults. **You can work to prevent inflammation by reducing the quantity of plant molecules you put into your body** and reducing the heat in your body by slowing it down. Using products like low dose naltrexone, which also reduces inflammation, and CBD oil, along with acupuncture, massage, meditation, light therapy, and visualization can be very beneficial.

"Inflammation is linked to nearly all of our diseases."

How Inflammation Affects the Body

BRAIN

Pro-inflamatory cytokines cause autoimmune reactions in the brain, which can lead to depression, autism, poor memory, Alzheimer's disease and MS.

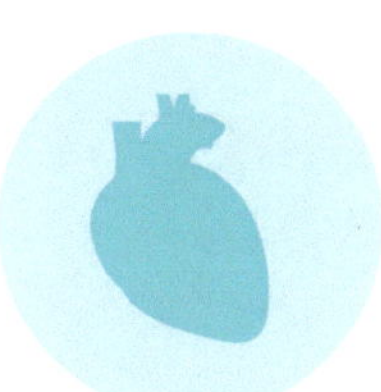

HEART

Inflammation in the heart & arterial & venous walls contributes to heart disease, strokes, high blood sugar (diabetes) and anemia.

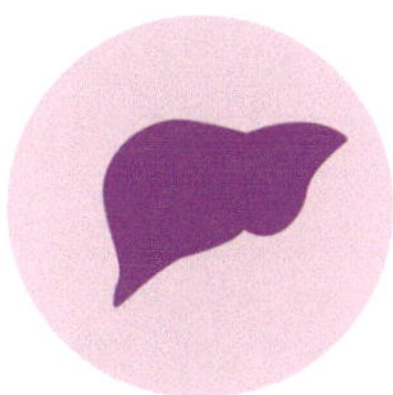

LIVER

Build-up of inflammation leads to an enlarged liver or fatty liver disease. Increased toxic load build-up in the body.

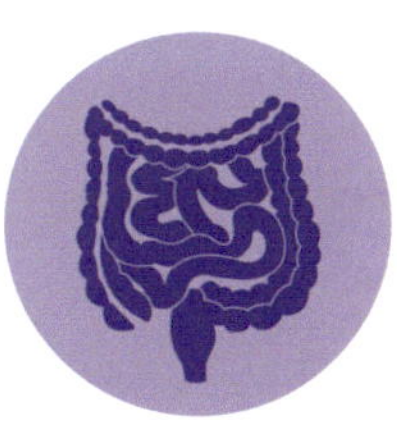

GI TRACT

Chronic inflammation damages our intestinal lining and can result in issues like GERD, Crohn's disease and Celiac disease. and MS.

BONES

Inflammation interferes with the body's natural ability to repair bone mass, increasing the number of fractures & leading to conditions like osteoporosis.

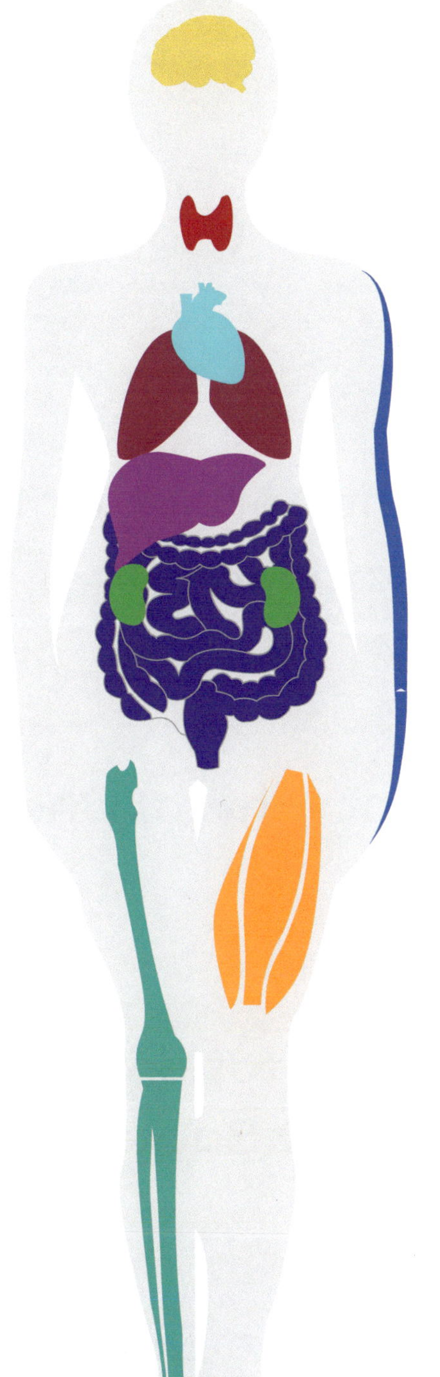

THYROID

Autoimmunity as a result of inflammation can reduce total thyroid receptor count & disrupts thyroid hormone function.

SKIN

Chronic inflammation compromises the liver & kidneys, resulting in rashes, dermatitis, eczema, acne, psoriasis, wrinkles & fine lines.

MUSCLE

Pro-inflamatory cytokines cause autoimmune reactions in the brain, which can lead to depression, autism, poor memory, Alzheimer's disease and MS.

KIDNEYS

Inflammatory cytokenis restrict blood flow to the kidneys. Complications like edema, hypertension, nephritis & kidney failure can result.

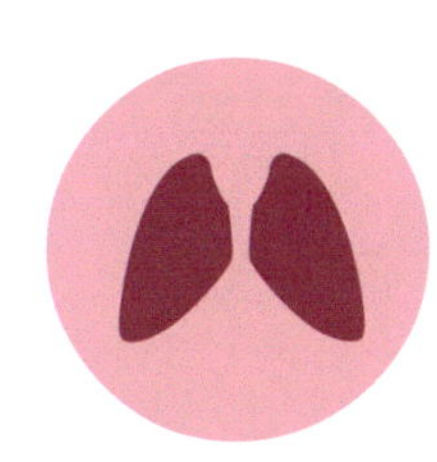

LUNGS

Inflammation induces autoimmune reactions against the linings of airways. Can result in allergies or asthma.

5 Causes of Inflammation

1. Glucose (Plant Sugars)

2. Plant Antinutrients & Antigens

3. Plant (Phyto) Chemicals

4. Fermentation of Fiber & Sugar by Yeast & Bacteria in the Gut

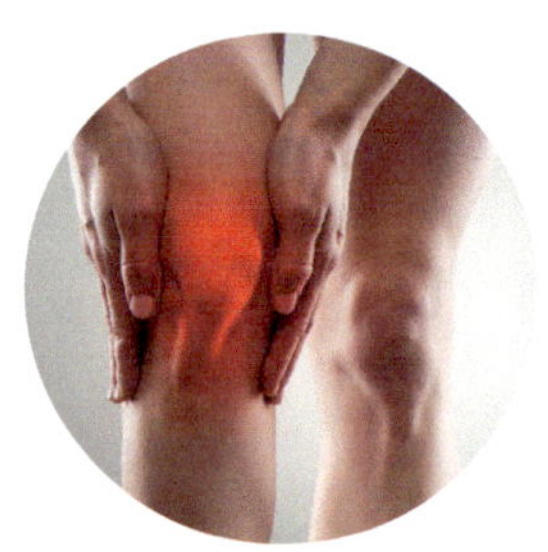

5. Excessive Exercise = Heat, Friction, & Damage

1.Glucose (Plant Sugars)

Glucose is a tasty fuel that we're driven to consume and eat in abundance. The human body is really smart. It has happy little sensors that say, "Wow! This makes me feel good!" It knows how to get you to eat. It knows how to get you fat because you are meant to be fat. We're driven to eat all carbohydrates, and some are more sugary and sweet for a reason: to get us fat-fuel filled.

If you're eating the standard diet, you're likely consuming 70% carbs, about 20% protein, and about 10% fat, mostly in the form of plant oils, including what we consider health fats—olive oil, coconut oi, and avocado oil, which may not be as healthy as animal fats.. They are industrialized, man-made oils, not nature's fat like that found on beef cattle or pigs. If this is how you're eating, you're producing a steady stream of glucose that is constantly fed into the blood stream and transported around the body.

As you feed the recommended 3-6 times per day, you're keeping your bowels always filled with digesting carbs, which simplify to simple sugars—which proves the hepatic portal system and thus the liver with glucose/sugar 24/7/365. Glucose is always fed to the liver where it's converted to fat. This requires insulin. If glucose is always elevated, so must insulin. There is no such thing as insulin resistance. Most if not all type 2 diabetes is created by simply eating too often and mostly all sugar (in the form of carbs and plants breaking down into mostly sugar). When you fast for at least 24 hours or more, your G.I. tract stops delivering sugar/glucose to your hepatic portal vein allowing glucose and insulin levels to drop, and you essentially go into a ketosis state. That is, as glucose drops, ketones show up. Our body is always making ketones from Acetyl COA, which is the breakdown of fatty acids and triglycerides, which are in abundance always! Anorexics are at risk of sudden death due to a lack of (necessary) fat. Obesity is associated with chronic illness (diabetes, hypertension, gout, coronary heart disease, cancer), due to a high carb/high sugar diet that is converted to fat—as it is meant to be. Symptoms of hypoglycemia are built in to our brains to get us to eat sugar. They are not life threatening. Your body makes all the sugar it needs and never has a requirement for an external source. We DON'T need to eat sugar ever! There are only essential fatty acids and amino acids. Glucose/sugars/glycans are a requirement for glycosylation—to make molecules functional in our bodies.

When you have a continuous supply of sugar molecules in your system, they bombard the body's cells like a meteor shower—binding themselves to fats and proteins in a process known as glycation. This forms advanced glycation end products (commonly and appropriately known as AGEs), which cause protein fibers to become stiff and malformed. Much of what is known about glycation's destructive effects comes from diabetes research. AGEs affect just about every organ system in the body, most conspicuously the skin. Glucose can make cells abnormal and cause the mitochondria to die or convert to tumors or cancer cells. Proteins found in the skin, namely collagen and elastin, are prone to glycation which results in discoloration, wrinkles, saggy skin, and a dull appearance that we frequently associate with aging.

Unfortunately, glycation is an inevitability. It happens to all of us, and its cumulative effect begins to show up around the age of 30-35. You can blame refined sugar, but it isn't the only culprit. Whole grains, fruits, and vegetables all turn to glucose when digested too, so they are also at fault.

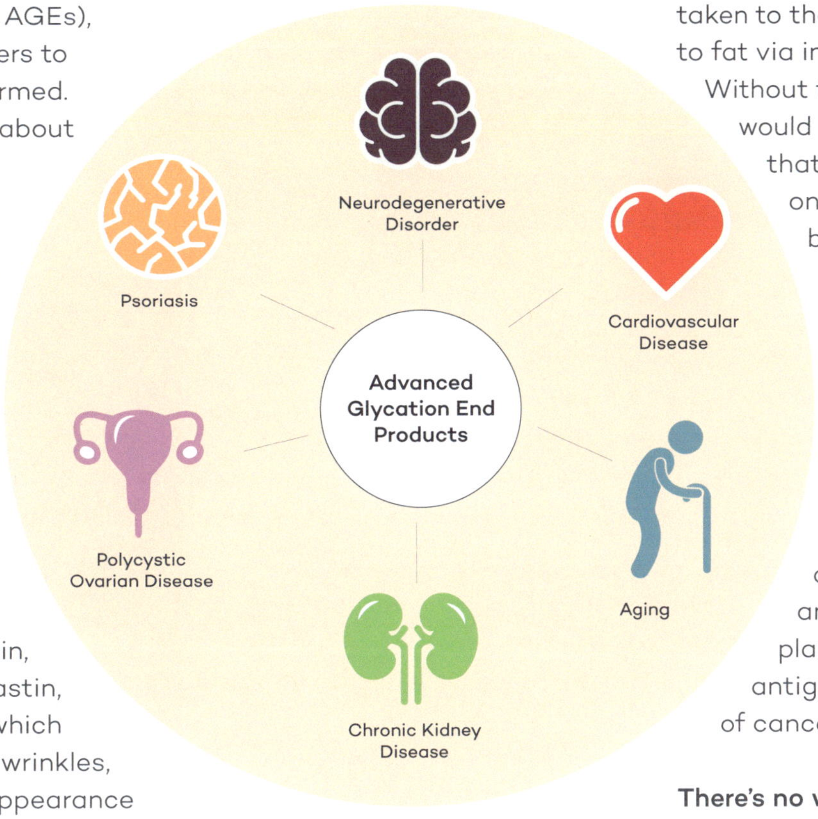

Advanced Glycation End Products
Neurodegenerative Disorder
Cardiovascular Disease
Aging
Chronic Kidney Disease
Polycystic Ovarian Disease
Psoriasis

In short, glucose kills mitochondria. Mitochondria are the essential energy factories for our cells, like mini turbines. They produce the energy that runs our cells. That energy is called ATP (Adenosine triphosphate). made from fatty acids.

When a person eats more food, they will produce more energy in the form of fat and store it for future use. That is our fat stores and our only cellular energy. You produce less energy, and you accumulate more fat. The more sugar you eat, the more damage is caused to the mitochondria. Over time, you may actually lose mitochondria. At that point, you are almost locked into a lower energy state. Unless you can stimulate the growth of more mitochondria to allow you to get back to your original energy level.

Fat is the fuel for the body. All sugar and amino acids must be taken to the liver and converted to fat via insulin in the liver cells. Without that conversion, we would not live. It is unlikely that our cells utilize glucose on a routine basis. It may be true when they're damaged or there's nothing else for a short amount of time—they're able to convert sugar to energy (ATP), but also other toxic products and lactic acid. Cancer cells thrive and survive on sugar, and likely sugar and other plant phytochemicals and antigens are the causes of cancer.

There's no way to completely stop glycation, but avoiding carbohydrates and sugars can help slow the proces.

FAT IS THE ONLY FUEL FOR YOUR BODY! FAT = ENERGY. YOU MUST CONVERT MOST SUGAR AND AMINO ACIDS TO FAT TO BE ALIVE. SUGAR AND AMINO ACIDS ARE NOT DIRECT FUELS FOR THE MITOCHONDRIA.

2. Plant Antinutrients & Antigens

"A lot of our chronic diseases are a result of toxic build-up of a species inappropriate diet and lack of species-specific nutrition, namely too many plants and not enough meat."
—Dr. Anthony Chaffee

Plant antinutrients and antigens are plant compounds that interfere with our ability to absorb vitamins and minerals and other nutrients, and damage our intestinal lining, triggering an inflammatory response in the G.I. tract and all over the body. They are found in most plant-based foods– particularly grains, beans, legume, nuts, and seeds. Antinutrients include things like phytic acid, leptins, and saponins.

You probably don't think of grains (wheat, barley, rye) as being seeds, but all grains are really the seeds of cereal grasses. Their antinutrients repel pests and bugs that can harm their development. They are part of the plant's immune system, but they also pose a problem for humans, making them a threat to our health..

Additionally, **the vitamins in the plants aren't nearly as bio-available as those in meats,** which means not as many nutrients are absorbed. Even some plants that are higher in nutrients (like spinach) don't result in that many nutrients being absorbed into the body due to the presence of antinutrients. Plants chelate and bind to the vitamins and minerals, inhibiting their absorption and causing deficiencies. Animal proteins don't have this problem. You are able to absorb almost all the nutrients.

If you choose to include seeds in your diet, it is best to soak, sprout, or ferment the seeds prior to consuming. This helps to reduce the concentration of antinutrients so they are less problematic. While the safest option may be eliminating the likely culprit from your diet, finding less antinutrient/antigenic foods, better preparing these foods before eating, or eating them less frequently. I understand many are reluctant to draw that line.

Second best would be eating locally grown, in season organic fruits that are ripe and focusing on seed-bearing fruits rather than eating the seeds themselves.

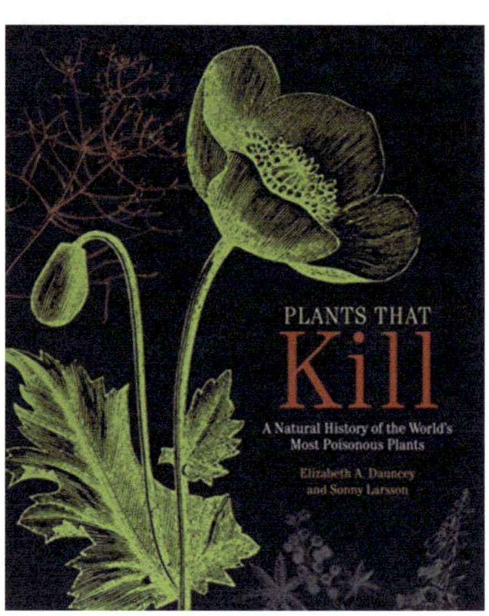

10 ANTINUTRIENTS TO AVOID

1. Phytic Acid (also called Phytate)
2. Gluten
3. Tannins
4. Oxalates
5. Lectins
6. Saponins
7. Trypsin Inhibitors
8. Isoflavaones
9. Solanine
10. Chaconine

Lectins: Particularly dangerous antinutrients are lectins. Lectins are a type of carbohydrate-binding protein that stick to cell membranes in the digestive tract and throughout our bodies. Humans are unable to digest lectins, so they travel through our gastrointestinal tract completely unchanged. **Foods high in lectins include nightshade vegetables (tomatoes, potatoes, goji berries, peppers, and eggplant), all legumes (lentils, beans, peanuts, and chickpeas), peanut-based products such as peanut butter and peanut oil, all grains and products made with grains or flour, and many dairy products including milk.** Cooking these foods can help to limit the effects of the lectins. Lectins are found in many foods, but nightshades, legumes, and grains are the biggest culprits. To add insult to injury, in our efforts to maximize crop yields, the agriculture industry has genetically modified many fruits and vegetables, which has caused them to express even more lectins.

Cellular Disruption:
One of the most concerning aspects about lectins is that they can cause cellular disruption. They can block transmissions between cells disrupting communication and resulting in brain fog and decreased mental performance. Lectins can also block or alter the messaging between hormone receptors resulting in endocrine disruption.

Oxalates: **Oxalates can attach to cells throughout the body leading to the disruption of the normal function of nerves,** glands, bones, and other cells. They are also known to prevent calcium absorption. Oxalates can become problematic if they over accumulate inside our body. The likely location for this overaccumulation is in our kidneys which, given the right circumstances, can lead to the formation of kidney stones.

Foods with the highest concentration of oxalates include rhubarb, spinach, beet greens, almonds, Swiss chard, cashews, and peanuts. The leaves of plants almost always contain higher oxalate levels than the roots, stems, and stalks. And unfortunately, oxalates aren't easily "cooked out" of foods and there is little you can do to rid them from the fruits and vegetables in which they are contained.

When we blend up fruits and veggies to make those "healthy" green smoothies and shakes, the end result is an oxalate smoothie. Even though some of the green veggies have valuable nutrients, the oxalates prevent our bodies from absorbing them.

PLANTS ARE NOT PART OF AN OPTIMAL HUMAN DIET

 **CONTAINS NUTRIENTS?**

 **ANY VITAL NUTRIENTS NOT FOUND IN MEAT?**

 **CAUSE HARM?**

PLANTS ARE TRYING TO KILL YOU. EAT MEAT.

Plants are out to get us. It sounds crazy, but it's true. Plants contain thousands of toxins and defense chemicals (aka poisons) geared toward preventing animals, insects, and pathogens from eating them.

- **70 people a year still die from eating potatoes!** The solanine in potatoes can be highly toxic.
- **Brussels Sprouts alone contain over 136 identified human carcinogens**
- Whitecap mushrooms have over 100 known carcinogens
- **Carbs change us metabolically, physically, and biologically,** but so do many plants we are eating on a regular basis. We're not realizing that plant chemicals cause a lot of harm and illness in humans and we don't treat it as such. We need to remove the toxins by removing the plants.

Estrogen
> 1m ng

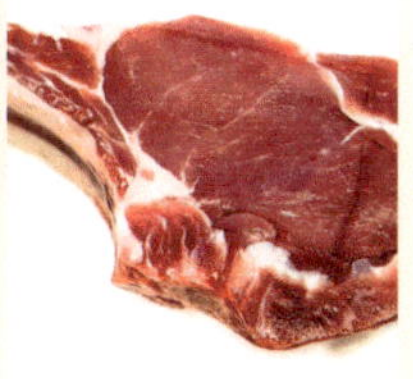

Estrogen
3.9 ng

HORMONE DISRUPTORS

PHYTOESTROGENS

Think hormones in meats are the problem? 3 oz. of soy contains more than 1 million nanograms of Estrogen, while 3 oz of lean red meat (in hormone treated cows) contains just 3.9 ng. Birth control pills typically contain about 35,000 ng. Fertile women make over 100,000 ng of estrogen a day.

3. Plant Chemicals that Kill (Phytochemicals)

What are plant phytochemicals? These are the nutrients often concentrated in the skins of many fruits and vegetables that are responsible for their color, hue, scent, and flavor. **Examples of foods rich in phytochemicals include: tomatoes, red onions, green tea, grapes, red cabbages, sweet potatoes, broccoli, kale, parsley, spinach, blueberries, raspberries, blackberries, melons, garlic, and the list goes on.** Plants produce phytochemicals to protect themselves from insect attacks and plant diseases. These compounds belong to four major categories: alkaloids, glycosides, polyphenols, and terpenes. They are also referred to as phytonutrients and are frequently touted as being essential nutrients that help to optimize health and fight cancer.

These phytochemicals we've been using as herbs and medicines to heal for thousands of years or to hurt as poisons. Herbal medicine was just the earliest form of the pharmaceutical industry. Native Americans and tribes in the Amazon have relied on "Medicine Men" or shamans to find natural remedies among the indigenous trees and plants. From using the bark of a tree to create an anesthetic or cure for malaria to using flowers to prevent the growth of tumors.

Approximately 7,000 medical compounds prescribed by Western doctors are derived from plants. Now we've figured out how to take those pharmaceuticals and grind them down, process them, separate them into their entities. For as many phytochemicals that are curative, there are also many which are addictive and deadly, namely heroin and cocaine, even marijuana. Unfortunately, the good aspects of plants can't always be isolated from the negative ones.

WHAT YOU DON'T KNOW ABOUT PLANTS:

- 99% of all plants in the world are inedible.
- Nearly 100% of animals are edible.
- Plants are designed for survival. We think we are using them, but they are really using us.
- 99.9% of all pesticides in our diets are natural chemicals in plants, produced to deter predators from eating them (including humans!), they're not chemicals sprayed by farmers!

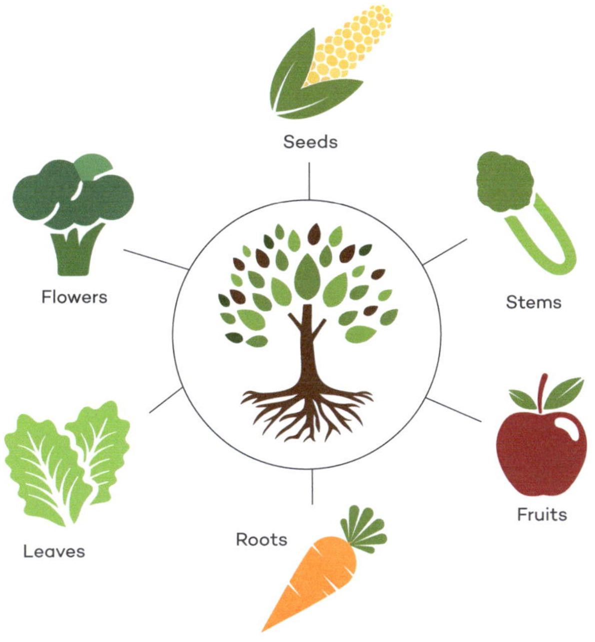

Flowers: cauliflower, broccoli, artichoke

Seeds: corn, peas, lima bean, string bean, legumes, peanuts, nuts

Stems: celery, asparagus, rhubarb

Fruits: pumpkin, cucumber, apple, tomato, eggplant, peppers, squash

Roots: carrots, radishes, potatoes, beets, turnips, sweet potatoes

Leaves: cabbage, lettuce, spinach

WHAT PART OF THE PLANT ARE YOU EATING?

Humans eat every part of plants from the seeds and roots to the stem and flowers. Many of us don't know which is which or that each part of a plant comes with its own particular plant poisons. Seeds are some of the riskiest because they represent the reproductive capabilities of the plant so they have lots of mechanisms to help ensure the continuation of the species.

And surprising as it may be, any grains that you're eating (wheat, corn, oats, and rice – pretty much any breakfast cereal) are the seeds of grasses. Nuts are the seeds of trees like walnuts, hazelnuts and pecans. And beans are the seeds of legumes like peas, lentils, soybeans, and chickpeas.

In 1907, in Australia, over 700 cattle died from eating the poisonous invasive plant 'Spiny Cocklebur' (Xanthium spinosum).

POISONOUS PLANTS

If you doubt the effects of phytochemicals are real, consider this example of sheep in Australia. Back in the 1940s, several farmers discovered "clover disease" in their populations of grazing sheep. Sheep who ate from fields of subterranean and red clover in turn developed infertility that caused lambing rates to drop by 60%–80%.

The clover species they were eating contained hormonally active phytochemicals (HAPs), particularly phytoestrogens. An ewe affected by clover disease can develop mammary gland hypertrophy, infertility, cervical deformities preventing conception, a prolapsed uterus (the uterus falls out through the vulva), or difficulty lambing.

TYPES OF PHYTOCHEMICALS

Carotenoids
Polyphenols
Flavonoids
Anthocyanins
Lignans
Indole-3-carbinol
Isoflavones
Resveratrol

4. Sugar + Fiber + Bacteria + Yeast = Fermentation (aka Alcohol)

Fibers are complex carbohydrates and strands of poorly or non-digestible carbs that essentially fuel the fire of the bowels. Fiber is like steel wool in our gastrointestinal tract and sandpaper in the gut. It damages and destroys the very sensitive mucosal lining of the gastrointestinal tract that is meant to be cared for in a delicate manner.

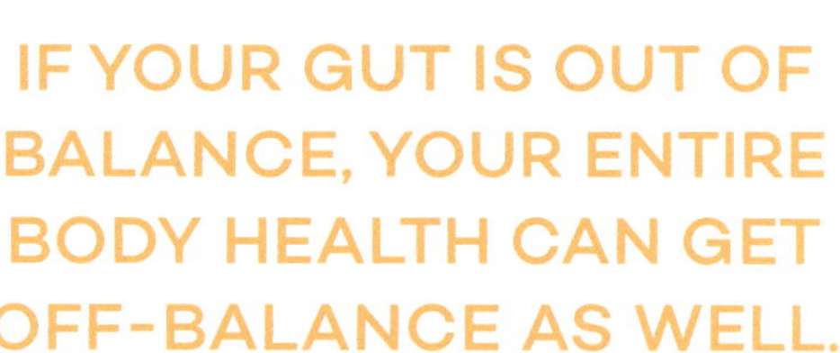

IF YOUR GUT IS OUT OF BALANCE, YOUR ENTIRE BODY HEALTH CAN GET OFF-BALANCE AS WELL.

We have been given the recommendations to fill the gut with poorly or non-digestible fiber (carbohydrates) that add bulk to the diet, push along the bowels, and help improve the daily constitutional or elimination. But, in fact, fiber may be adding to the damage and disease by fueling the bacteria and yeast with the food they love, which ultimately breaks down to sugar. When you chew fiber, you simplify it and expose it to enzymes which break it down during the process of digestion. **But fiber creates heat, gas, aldehyde, alcohol, and methane.** It's bad for the bowels. It's pushing down to create hemorrhoids. It's pushing up to produce GERD, and eventually all of that inflammation causes disease.

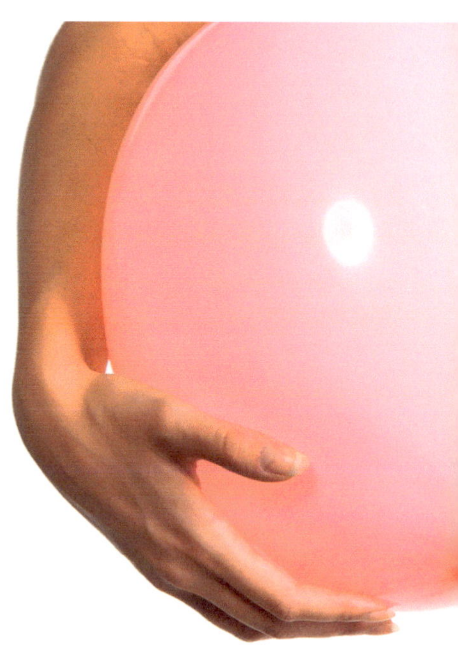

The fiber gets down to the colon where it adds bulk to enlarge the feces in order to make it more difficult to get through the small exit portal. We have been given advice by health care practitioners and nutritionists to eat lots of fiber, but quite possibly (and likely) doing so is having the opposite effect on our health. Fiber fuels the fire of inflammation. Bacteria and yeast love it.

Bacteria and yeast make heat, alcohol, and aldehydes that fuel the inflammatory processes in the body leading to colitis, irritable bowel, Crohn's, hemorrhoids, cancer, you name it. Gas is bad. Alcohol is made in the colon, the rectum, and the digestive tract, which basically travels to every cell of our body and damages the body even more.

The immense number of bowel surgeries and bowel problems people are experiencing as a result are overwhelming. A high vegan/vegetarian, plant-based diet sounds like it's the healthiest thing for us, but I believe it's likely doing more harm than good. There's an increasing body of research studying the Gut-Brain Axis. The gut is sometimes referred to as the body's "second brain" as it controls about 70% of your body's immune response. If your gut is out of balance, your entire body health can get off-balance as well.

My general recommendation is to eliminate all fruits, fiber, and vegetables. After reading Fiber Menace by Konstantin Monastyrsky, I had a better understanding of the danger of fiber. I didn't believe it until I eliminated the fruits and vegetables I thought were healthy, and my bowels became the best ever.

Our bodies are remarkable and amazing. Healing is their nature, but we can't heal if we're constantly feeding them inflammatory products (alcohol, fruits, fibers, vegetable) and a lack of fat.

FIBER IS LIKE STEEL WOOL IN OUR GASTROINTESTINAL TRACT AND SANDPAPER IN THE GUT.

Fiber + Fermentation= Bloated Belly / Bacteria / Yeast

5. EXCESSIVE EXERCISE = Heat, Friction, & Damage

EXCESSIVE EXERCISE = INFLAMMATION

Lots of us use exercise as a way to de-stress (and an opportunity to show off our strong bodies and abilities to create and protect like a mating call). That post-work run or spin class makes us feel good, productive, and provides an outlet for working out frustration with our boss, our spouse, or life in general. The endorphin rush feels great, so we put on our work out gear, lace up our sneakers, and hit the treadmill day after day.

Americans in particular seem trapped in a vicious cycle of eating way too much and then working out way too hard to burn all of the extra calories they've consumed. **We are a society of excesses for sure.** The common belief about exercise is that if a little is good, a lot must be great. Not so, unfortunately. When you exercise, you are heating up your body causing DNA and protein degradation, pain, swelling, friction, and more heat. It stimulates epinephrine and cortisol and steals blood flow from the core central organs. The kidneys and digestive track take a huge hit! Exercise and digestion tend to be mutually exclusive activities. When you exercise, your body doesn't use its energy for digestion. Instead, it slows any digestion currently taking place so it can divert as much blood as it can to feed your muscles and your lungs.

During exercise, the perfusion of blood increases to the lungs, myocardium, and skeletal muscles as it's re-routed from the kidneys and digestive tract. **Repetitive exercise increases the destruction of our bodies causing rapid damage and dysfunction.** Repetitive motion injuries are yet another concern – tennis elbow, runner's knee, tendonitis, just to name a few.

MY ADVICE: SLOW IT DOWN.

I say this to my clients, co-workers, and friends like a broken record. Get off the hamster wheel (my name for the treadmill), elliptical, and racing bike. Exercise raises endorphins, which is good, so don't sit still, but you don't have to be so intense with the exercise, which increases inflammation.

Walk instead of run. Remember the tortoise and the hare? Slow and steady may not win every race, but who wants to get to life's finish line first? The average life span of a tortoise is over 100 years with some species living almost twice that. Coincidence? I think not.

High impact exercise on a regular basis is bad for you. I'm not suggesting you sit still and become a couch potato. Intentional movement is important. **But there are other ways to de-stress that are less harmful to your body: yoga, meditation, Tai Chi, walking, and light motion activity that is simple, easy, and regenerative.**

Go for a walk in the woods and connect with nature. Walk with a friend to catch up and reconnect. Do something creative that uses your mind and your body. Paint. Make pottery. Make jewelry. Write. Sing. Dance. Do something that inspires you every day, These types of activities allow the flow of blood to the core, brain, and bowels where it's needed and don't create an immune reaction that is more damaging and destructive. A 2017 study from Alimentary Pharmacology and Therapeutics found that as exercise intensity and duration rise, the likelihood of intestinal injury increases.

WHEN YOU EXERCISE, YOU ARE HEATING UP YOUR BODY CAUSING DNA AND PROTEIN DEGRADATION, PAIN, SWELLING, FRICTION, AND MORE HEAT.

Believe it or not, dancing is a great choice and can reverse the signs of aging on the brain and improve physical health. On top of strengthening the area of your brain involved with memory (hippocampus), dancing also improves endurance, flexibility, balance and body coordination—all great things especially in an aging population.

Again, we need to take our cue from the king of the jungle. Lions don't exercise! Yes, they move a little bit. They hunt. They feast, feed, and reproduce. All animals do. We've got to get back to the fact that we are a human animal that requires breathing, eating, drinking, and reproducing. And we require the protection and presence of the herd and connections to others. These connections vibrate in a positive way.

Good Excercise	Bad Excercise
Yoga	Treadmill
Tai Chi	Spinning Class
Pilates	Speedwork on Track
Barre	Heavy Weightlifting
Walking	Cross-Fit
Casual Bike Ride	Endurance Training
Gentle Weights	
Resistance Bands	

High-Fat Low to No Carb Eating & Fasting Reduces Inflammation

A high-fat, low carb diet (ideally animal-based) helps reduce inflammation through five primary mechanisms:

It reduces carbohydrate intake. Carbohydrates cause inflammation.

It reduces plant toxins. Plant toxins cause inflammation.

It reduces the ingestion of bacteria and other antigens. Bacteria causes inflammation.

It reduces fiber. Fiber causes inflammation.

It increases the ingestion of fats. Fats reduce inflammation.

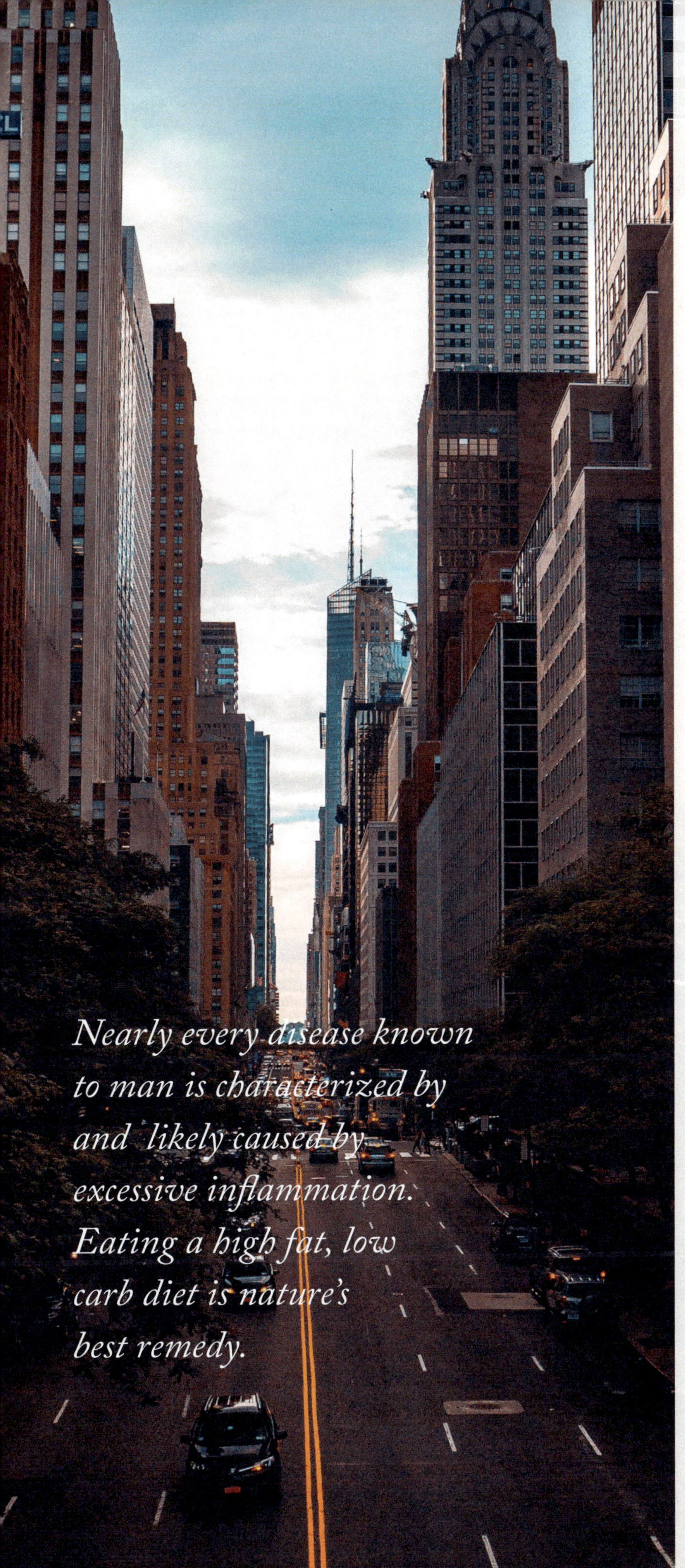

Nearly every disease known to man is characterized by and likely caused by excessive inflammation. Eating a high fat, low carb diet is nature's best remedy.

Diseases of Western Civilization

According to the World Health Organization, people who live in high-income countries and middle-income countries predominantly die of chronic "lifestyle" diseases or "diseases of civilization."

- Type 2 Diabetes
- Autoimmune Diseases
- Asthma
- Alzheimer's Disease
- Acne
- Atherosclerosis
- Coronary Heart Disease
- Cerebrovascular Disease
- Peripheral Vascular Disease
- Stroke
- Obesity
- Hypertension
- Gallstones
- Fatty Liver Disease
- Cancer
- Alcoholism
- Gout
- Allergies
- Depression
- Diverticulitis
- Osteoporosis

Benefits of Cholesterol

Over the past several decades, cholesterol has gotten a bad rap. Fear of high cholesterol levels on bloodwork panels during annual physicals steered us away from eating too many eggs and fatty meats and toward lean proteins and man-made fats like margarine and vegetable oil. In truth, eggs, fatty meats, and butter don't raise cholesterol levels in our bodies. It's really eating diets high in sugar and carbs. Our bodies need cholesterol to function correctly. **Cholesterol helps us to maintain proper hormone function and fight inflammation.** The liver makes about 75% of the cholesterol we need, but we need to take in the remaining 25% through our diet. And the primary source for this additional cholesterol is animal fats.

Cholesterol is a necessary building block of **growth and development**, so important that breast milk from a healthy mother has about 50 to 60 percent of its energy (kilocalories) as fat. The cholesterol in breast milk supplies an infant with close to six times the amount most adults consume. This is especially important during infancy-- the most rapid period of growth and development we experience as humans.

1 Cholesterol, along with saturated fats, **gives our cells required stiffness and stability.** When the diet contains an excess of polyunsaturated fats (vegetable oils or omega-6) instead of saturated fats in the cell membrane, the cell walls become flabby. If this happens, cholesterol from the blood drives into the tissues to give them structural integrity. This is why serum cholesterol levels may go down temporarily when we replace saturated fats with polyunsaturated fats in the diet.

2 **Cholesterol is vital for production and function of serotonin receptors in the brain.** Serotonin is the body's "feel-good" chemical. Low cholesterol levels have been linked to depression and aggression. Anti-depressants often don't work for patients who are eating a vegetarian diet.

3 **Mother's milk is VERY high in cholesterol** and has an important enzyme that assists the baby in using this nutrient. Babies and children need foods high in cholesterol to guarantee proper development of the brain and nervous system (BUT we also need these as adults!!!)

4 Cholesterol acts as a precursor to important hormones that **help us deal with stress and protect the body against cancer and heart disease.** It is also important to our sex hormones like androgen, testosterone, estrogen and progesterone. Which is why women trying to get pregnant have more success on a high saturated fat diet!

5 Cholesterol is necessary for us to use vitamin D; which is an essential fat-soluble vitamin needed for healthy bones and nervous system, insulin production, reproduction and immune system function, proper growth, mineral metabolism, and muscle tone.

6 Bile is vital for digestion and assimilation of fats in the diet; which is made from cholesterol that we eat.

7 Current studies are now showing that **cholesterol performs as an antioxidant,** which is why cholesterol levels go up with age. As an antioxidant, it protects us against free radical damage that leads to heart disease and cancer.

8 **Dietary cholesterol helps maintain the health of the intestinal wall.** People on low-cholesterol vegetarian diets often develop leaky gut syndrome and other intestinal disorders.to heat and oxygen.

CELL MEMBRANE

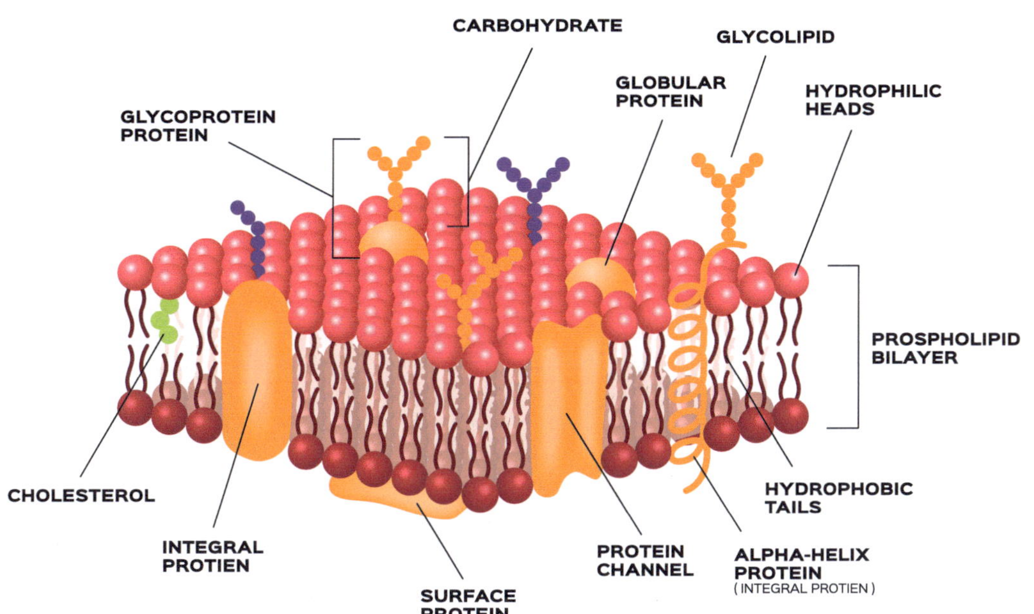

Cholesterol plays a significant role in the function of the cell membrane, which has the highest concentration of cholesterol,with around 25-30% of lipids in the cell membrane being cholesterol.

Cholesterol can become damaged by exposure to heat and oxygen. This oxidized cholesterol tends to promote damage to the arterial cells and cause buildup of plaque in the arteries. Damaged cholesterol is found in powdered milk; which is added to reduced-fat milks to give them body. That is why I NEVER suggest drinking skim milk! It is also found in powdered eggs and in meats that have been heated to high temperatures in frying and other high-temperature processes. So fast food items come into play here.

Hypothyroidism can result in high cholesterol levels. When thyroid function is poor, usually due to a diet low in usable iodine, fat-soluble vitamins and high in sugar, the blood gets filled with cholesterol as a protective mechanism, providing a large amount of minerals needed to heal tissues. Hypothyroid individuals are particularly susceptible to infections, heart disease and cancer.

Source: Maria Emmerich

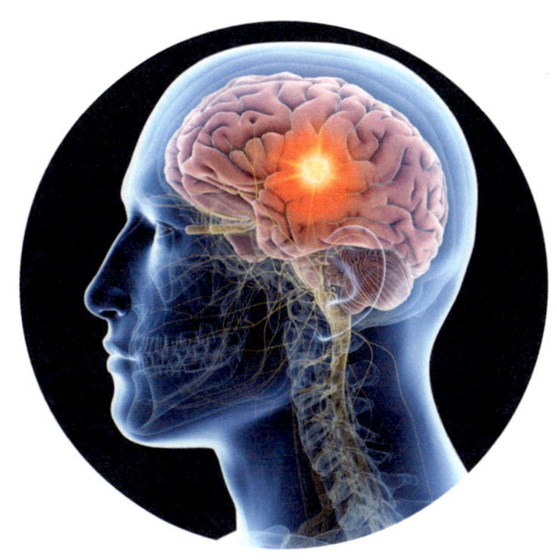

THE BRAIN IS MADE OF FAT AND CHOLESTEROL.

IF YOU SOMEHOW REMOVED ALL CHOLESTEROL, THE BODY WOULD MELT AND DISAPPEAR.

My advice:

STOP TRYING TO REDUCE YOUR CHOLESTEROL INTAKE. It does NOT cause disease. Your body is made of cholesterol. Your body is a fat-making and fat-burning machine.

Cholesterol Lies & Truths

"Cholesterol causes heart disease." **FALSE**

"Fat in your diet equals fat in your blood and fat on your body." **FALSE**

The mainstream theory that LDL causes coronary heart disease has been maintained by misleading statistics,exclusion of unsuccessful trials, and ignoring contradictory findings." **TRUE**

One topic of health and nutrition that has perpetuated more lies than truth is cholesterol. The genesis for much of the medical world's misinformation about cholesterol can be traced back to Ancel Keys, who in 1961, famously developed his cholesterol hypothesis. From his research, Keys concluded that the consumption of saturated fat leads to increased cholesterol that clogs arteries and leads to heart disease. Though his conclusions were not statistically sound, Keys' hypothesis became the basis for more than a half-century of medical and nutritional recommendations, which in turn have led to the demonization of fat and high use of statins.

After his own hypertriglyceridemia diagnosis Dr. David Diamond, a neuroscientist, decided to research statins and began investigating how his doctor and the dietary guidelines could have gotten the science on cholesterol so wrong. Diamond reviewed cholesterol science, Keys' findings, and statin research, concluding that, "People with high cholesterol have a significantly lower rate of cancer, infectious disease, and live [an] overall normal lifespan."

Many other researchers have come to the same conclusion. Keys constructed his hypothesis after studying the diets and heart disease in countries across the globe. But his research left out nations with data that did not match the hypothesis, and even within the data he published, populations existed in which diet and heart disease were outliers to his model. This cherry-picking of data is simply bad science.

Because he did not track information like sugar/carbohydrates consumption in the diet or even the contributions of exercise, smoking, exposure to environmental toxins, as well as other potential confounding variables, Keys' research is essentially meaningless.

It seems glaringly obvious to us today that smoking, exercise, and other lifestyle factors play a huge role in general health and the development of heart disease, but these issues were not recognized as important in the middle of the 20th century.

Since the release of the Keys' theory, there have not been any actual diet studies which support his theory with hard data. And in fact, the amount of dietary fat consumed in the United States has steadily declined over the last few decades, but coronary heart disease rates are still increasing.

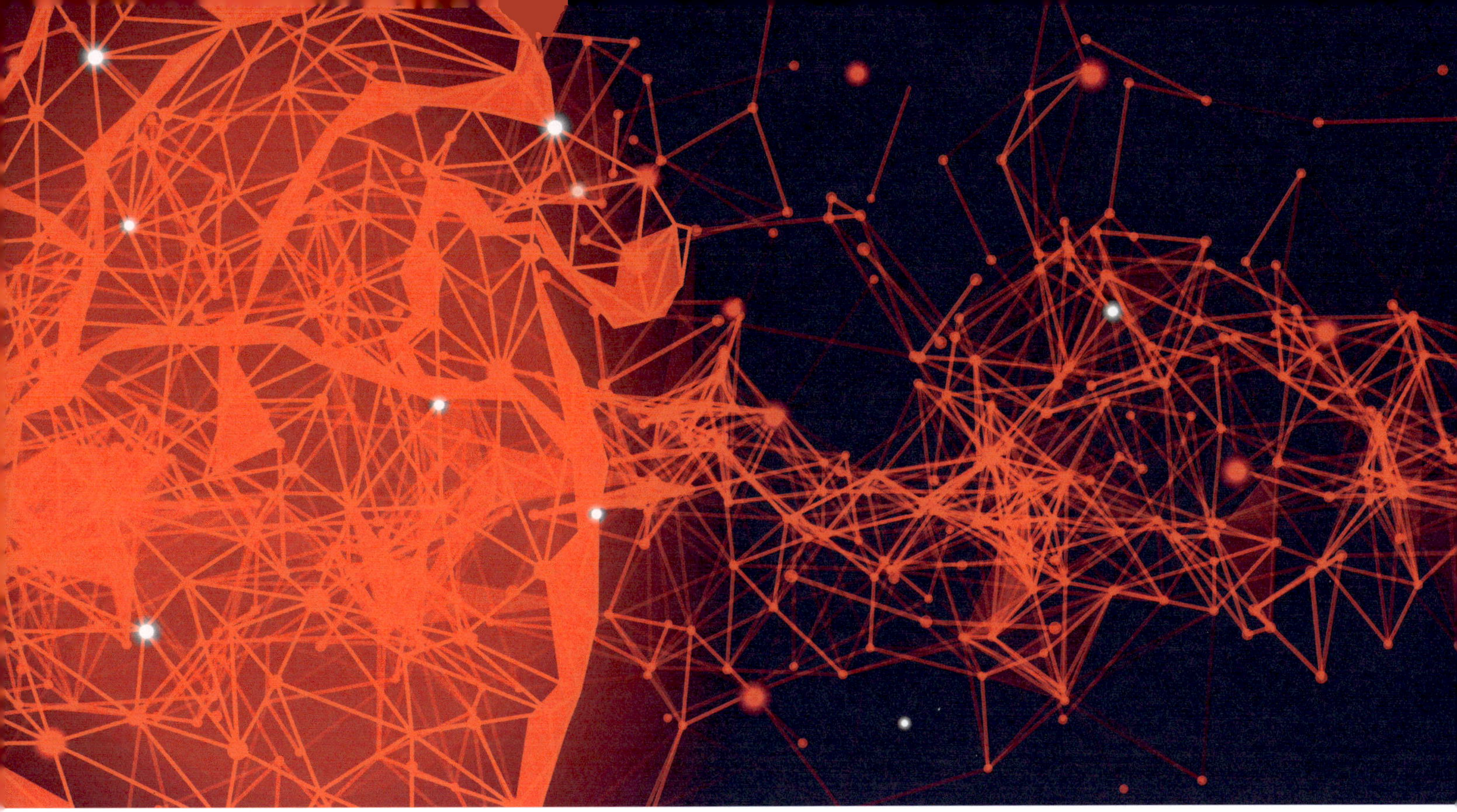

The Truth

CHOLESTEROL IS NOT YOUR ENEMY. PLANTS ARE.

IF NOT CHOLESTEROL, THEN WHAT CAUSES HEART DISEASE?

Cholesterol is not in and of itself dangerous and is absolutely essential to your body. We now know that sugar, not fat, is one of the largest contributors to coronary heart disease. Most of this damage comes from "metabolic syndrome", a precursor for diabetes.

"Unhealthy" levels of cholesterol in the body are not actually unhealthy, and about half of all heart attacks occur in people who don't have elevated levels of cholesterol. This alone is a huge red flag that should point us in another direction for finding out what causes coronary heart disease.

Unfavorable levels of lipoproteins (cholesterol carrying molecules) in the blood are generated by eating a diet high in sugar and carbohydrates. Eating a diet consistently high in carbohydrates and sugar causes changes to body chemistry which lead to "metabolic syndrome", diabetes, obesity, and then to heart disease.

Dr. Diamond and his research team concluded that while statin treatment may reduce cholesterol levels, they do not, in fact, substantially improve cardiovascular outcomes, and serious adverse effects of statin treatment are highly underestimated.

Approaches to improving cardiovascular outcomes that should be emphasized are stopping smoking, avoiding obesity, and consuming foods low in sugar and partially hydrogenated fats and high in saturated fats, such as coconut, butter, eggs and full fat cheese.

Glycation (Bad)

Picture what would happen if, instead of gasoline, you filled your car's gas tank with sugar. It's not the right fuel, will likely 'gum up' and mess up the functionality of the engine, and your car won't go as far as fast, if it even goes at all. This is what high levels of blood sugar can do to our bodies.

When blood sugar is very high, has nowhere to go, and your body isn't working well enough to get it out of the blood stream, it starts to stick to things it doesn't belong on. Red blood cells have lots of proteins and those proteins flow easily and effortlessly in the blood stream. But when sugar gloms onto those proteins, they get "sticky" and it gets harder for them to move, particularly into smaller vessels like capillaries. This is one of the reasons we see diabetics experience trouble with their eyes, kidneys, and big toes. These areas are all fed by tiny capillaries. When blood sugar is constantly elevated, it sticks onto these proteins (this is called GLYCATION), and you end up with sticky blood that doesn't flow easily through small openings. Glycated proteins form clusters called AGEs (Advance Glycation End-Products). We want to reduce these. One of the most effective ways to reduce glycation and the stickiness in our blood stream is to not get our blood sugar so high. This is most easily accomplished by eating a low-carb diet.

Glycation affects all of the organs and tissues in our bodies. Glycation of the structural protein collagen in the heart can lead to heart failure. In bone, this can increase the risk of fractures. When glycation occurs to the protein elastin in the wall of the aorta, this can result in stiffness and high blood pressure. Glycation of proteins in the brain such as the beta amyloid protein increases the formation of the plaques which are the cause of Alzheimer's Disease. Glycation of proteins in the eye changes their shape and can reduce vision and lead to cataract formation. Glycation of certain growth factors can decrease healing with age. The presence of AGEs can trigger inflammatory reactions from the immune system, increasing chronic inflammation in the body.

The glycation of enzymes decreases enzyme function, which can lead the body to produce fewer antioxidants increasing oxidative stress within the body. This is like rusting from the inside out.

Heart disease, Alzheimer's, bad vision, reduced circulation . . . these are all symptoms we generally regard as a normal part of aging, but by reducing sugar in our blood stream, we can delay or avoid many of these problems.

Glycation is the abnormal binding of glycans that damage cellular organs and contribute to disease.

Glycations causes proteins and lipids to no longer function and even to become harmful to your body. **The good news is that while you can't stop glycation entirely, there are some ways to reduce the AGE load in your body**. In fact, diet is the biggest contributor of AGEs.

1. **Reduce sugar intake to as close to zero as possible.** Sugar feeds glycation. This means cutting out carbs that metabolize into sugar (bread, pasta, crackers, alcohol) and refined carbs. Read labels to find where sugar is "hidden" in dairy alternatives, sauces, marinades, etc.

2. AGEs can also form in foods. Foods that have been exposed to high temperatures and dry heat, such as grilling, roasting, baking, frying, sautéing, broiling, searing, and toasting tend to be very high in AGEs. **Choose cooking methods like boiling, steaming, poaching, and low temp cooking that don't brown** the foods. Browning is a reaction between proteins and sugar. Even if your diet appears to be reasonably healthy, you may consume an unhealthy amount of harmful AGEs just because of the way you're cooking your food.

3. **Light exercise can help reduce sugar stores by burning through excess sugar for energy.**

4. **Certain vitamins can help prevent glycation and help reverse the damage of AGEs.** Benfotiamine (B1 derivative) and B6 found in poultry, fish, and organ meats can trap the products of sugar break-down before glycation occurs.

5. **Vitamin C is a powerful antioxidant** and can help fight against glycation, which is why it's found in most supplements.

Glycocalyx: An Essential Barrier

It's likely you've never heard of it, but an essential element for your good health lies in the protective gel lining of our capillaries and vital organs that touches trillions of cells. Capillaries make up 99% of your circulatory system from head to toe. Every heartbeat delivers vital nutrients and oxygen while waste is removed from each cell. This process breaks down over time as a result of aging, poor diet, a lack of exercise, genetics, and stress.

Medical researchers have discovered the importance of this micro-thin gel-like lining of your blood vessels that protects your entire circulatory system. **The glycocalyx enables nutrient, hormone, and oxygen delivery, and waste and carbon dioxide removal, from vital organs.**

Blood vessels were originally assumed to be hollow tubes, but researchers have discovered that the entire circulatory system is protected by a gel like lining that protects the inside walls of the arteries, veins, and capillaries. It's like a Teflon coating, and it's called the endothelial glycocalyx. Glyco means sugar, and calyx, refers to a fibrous sponge-like material. **The glycocalyx lining is continuously being produced to coat the inner lining cells.** It is composed of many compounds, but most of it is heparin (a blood thinner) and chondroitin sulfate (a slick substance that's found in your joints). The glycocalyx is made up of sugar and protein. They are hair-like structures that stick out from the artery wall. Blood flowing through vessels doesn't touch the vessel walls, instead it comes into contact with the glycocalyx.

The glycocalyx keeps your body healthy in three important ways:

1. **It stimulates the production of nitric oxide,** which is vital for controlling blood flow and blood pressure. The glycocalyx stores anti-oxidates, and by working in tandem with nitric oxide, can increase blood flow on-demand when organs need it. Your body needs a thick and healthy glycocalyx to regulate blood flow.

2. **It allows your body to engage more capillaries when needed.** Your body's level of activity dictates when this is necessary. When you're active, your organs need more nourishment and faster waste removal.

3. **It is composed of strands of sugars and proteins bound together.** This results in a thick, sticky layer that helps cells stay put in environments with a lot of physical stress.

It's not only the vascular system that has glycocalyx. The gut also uses has this protective barrier. Microvilli cells in the small intestine are covered by a glycocalyx, which protects the cells from the acidic solution in the digestive tract and make up the glycobiome. But the glycocalyx can become damaged. Long-term or multiple courses of antibiotics typically erode the glycocalyx that normally coat the intestinal microvilli. **The good news is that this damage to the glycocalyx doesn't have to be permanent.** It's not too late to slow or even reverse glycocalyx breakdown.

One of the easiest ways of supporting a healthy glycocalyx is eating an anti-inflammatory diet (like carnivore), reducing stress, and regular movement (walking, stretching, yoga, Tai Chi).

Lifestyle factors that degrade the endothelial glycocalyx include smoking, a high sugar diet, lack of physical activity, stress, air pollution, aging, and systemic inflammation. A healthy glycocalyx is key to preventing heart attacks and strokes.

Healthy vs. Compromised Glycocalyx

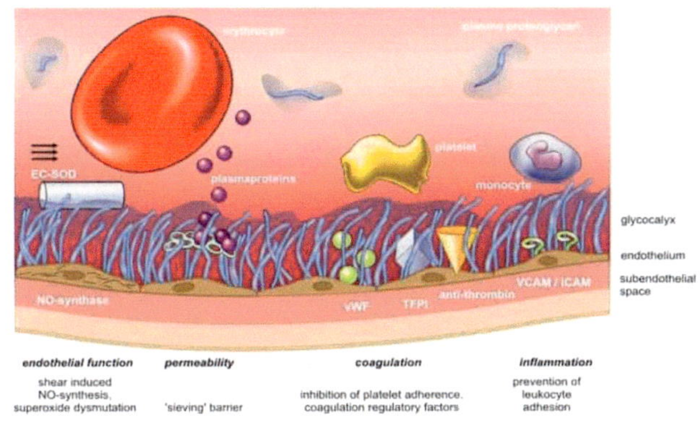

Compromised

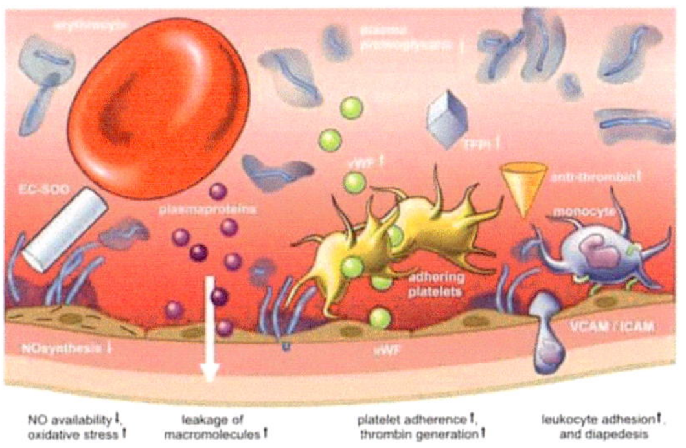

Foreign sugars, glycans from plants, and other microbes (bacteria/yeast /viruses) cause inflammation and are responsible for most diseases.

The Glycobiome: Our Body's Sugar Code

WHAT IS THE GLYCOBIOME & WHY IT'S IMPORTANT TO YOUR HEALTH

Inside our bodies simple sugar molecules connect to create powerful structures that have only recently been linked to various health problems like cancer, aging, and autoimmune diseases. These long sugar chains that cover each of our cells are called glycans, and researchers believe that creating a map of their location and structure has the potential to help doctors diagnose and treat a variety of diseases. These glycans are part of the human glycobiome – the entire collection of sugars within our body.

This cellular "sugar coating" has been a mystery until recently when researchers began to catalog the hundreds of thousands of sugars and their locations on various cell types, with the goal of using this information to tailor medical therapies to each individual.

Glycans - are simple and complex sugars that bind to proteins and lipids (glycosylation) to create proper functionality.

Glycosylation – the normal binding of a glycan (sugar) to a protein to make functional.

WHAT DO GLYCANS DO?

The main job of glycans is to influence the proteins and fats that sit on the surface of our cells. Together, they create a thick sugar coat around the cell. You can think of the surface of a cell as soil and the glycans are like the trees and plants that bring color and identity to the cell. If you were able to see a cell with your naked eye, it would look very fuzzy.

Glycans are critical for glycosolation--adding a sugar to a protein to make it functional.

Scientists predict that in the near future, we'll use glycans to predict individual risk for certain diseases (the same way we use genes today). Along with DNA, proteins, and fats, glycans are one of the four major macromolecules essential for life. Of these four, glycans are the final decision-maker for how our cells behave. Glycans have the ability to change how our cells respond to stimuli. For example, if you alter a few glycans on the outside of a cell, it might trigger that cell to move to a different location within the body.

Glycobiome alterations can be specifically tied to particular diseases. Also, biological processes like aging are linked to inflammation in our glycobime. Researchers don't yet know whether reversing these changes will allow us to prevent certain diseases or slow the aging process.

FRIEND OR FOE?

Every single cell in the human body is covered with a collection of glycans which are assembled using various simple sugars like glucose, mannose, galactose, sialic acid, glucosamine and fructose as building blocks. The glycobiome of a particular cell reflects its unique gene expression pattern. It is how cells know YOU are YOU! By sensing the type of sugar coat present, our immune cells are able to identify other cells as friend or foe. This is because bacteria have sugars on their surfaces that are never seen on human cells – the pathogen's sugars are sensed by the immune system which allow it to identify the bacteria as 'foreign.'

The mucosa-associated microbes are particularly important for nutrient exchange, communication with the host, development of the immune system, and resistance against invading pathogens.

The glycobiome is how the body interacts with the environment and how the cells interact with each other.

COLLOQUIAL WAYS TO UNDERSTAND THE GLYCOBIOME:

The sugars we eat or make (and we can make what we need) are used by the body to provide building blocks for glycosylation and glycation, which tell us the following:

1. This is my cell or this is not my cell. The glycobiome of a particular cell reflects its unique gene expression pattern. It is how cells know YOU are YOU! Viruses and bacteria can mimic us so they can invade via glycation and glycosylation.
2. Cells in our immune systems express cell surface associated glycoproteins and glycolipids that together with Glycan Binding Proteins and other molecules sense environmental changes. In other words . . . is this a safe place to live or not?
3. Donor organs have carbohydrate antigens that trigger immune rejection – therefore understanding the glycome is critical to organ transplant programs

Some Diseases & Disorders we can make sense of when we understand the glycome

- Autoimmunity
- Chronic Inflammation
- Rheumatoid Arthritis
- Inflammatory Bowel Disease
- Systemic Lupus Erythematosus
- Tri Syndrome
- Granulomatosis with Polyangiitis
- IgA Nephropathy
- Diabetes Mellites

SO, WHAT'S THE STORY ABOUT THE GLYCOBIOME RELATIVE TO CARNIVORE?

Sugars are NOT for nutrition. Their role is regulatory, for signaling, cell-to-cell recognition or rejection, and translation of environmental cues for the organism to flounder or flourish.

A carnivore way of life does not reject a role for sugars, just the need to consume them as a source of energy, like muscle, which your body can use in a pinch for energy, but really you want to consume fats and proteins for that.

The enormous number of glycoconjugates (over 10,000,000,000,000) tells us that, like genetic combinations in DNA, sugars are part of the glycobiome and help animals to survive and prosper ... if used appropriately. Eating plants or sugars is not the way to get what you need (your body can provide it), especially considering the secondary deleterious effects of sugar on insulin function.

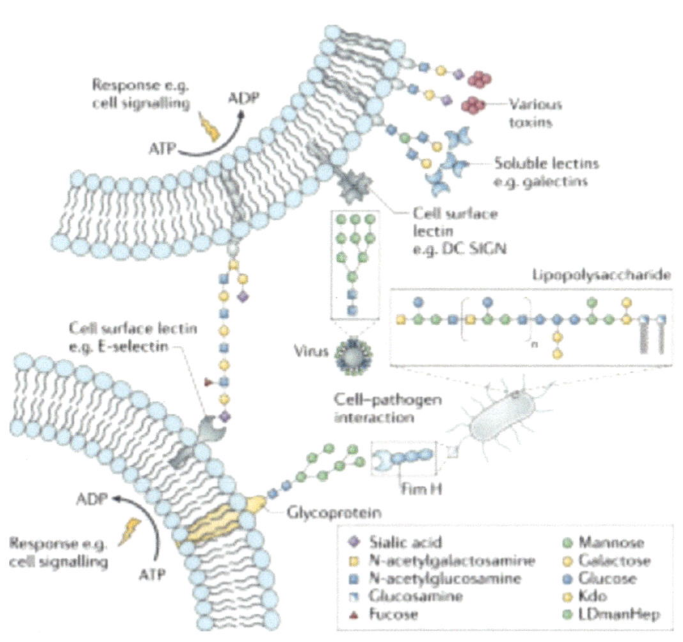

The Lymphatics

When we talk about health and wellness, people don't spend much time discussing the lymphatic system, yet it is critical to maintaining optimal health. When we eat fat, it lubricates the lymphatics, and acts like a solvent within the gut to micronize, capture and filter (via the lymph nodes) the waste residue that is brought in through the foods we eat. If we don't eat fat, many of those antigens get stuck in your gut where they can get into the submucosal layer and interstitial layer of the GI tract leading to inflammation.

While other antigens are delivered to the liver where they interfere with the blood system and pollute every nook and cranny of our bodies. This is an essential part of why a high carbohydrate / low fat diet is deadly. **Sugar causes glycation in the lymph system.** And since the lymph system does not have smooth muscle to help propel the lymphatic fluid, it relies on the natural flow and pressure of a system that's intact and lubricated by quality fat. Lymphangitis, lymph node swelling, lymphomas, and leukemia are rampant worldwide because of a low fat / high carb diet filled with excessive frequency, volume, and variety of sugar and carbohydrates.

Amazingly, the entire intrabdominal cavity, the left side of the chest, the left side of the face, and the lower extremities all dump into the thoracic duct. It's a huge collector of fluid and fat that needs to circulate and return back to your blood system.

Meanwhile, the lymphatic tissue is sent through lymph nodes that employ a filter system and immunologic system with white blood cells that identify the foreign particles and make antibodies against the antigens so that your body can react against them, clean them up, and be ready for the next barrage.

All of the fat in the GI tract goes to the lymphatics and the thoracic duct. The majority of the antigens and dirt dissolve in the fat.

When you eat the fat, it lubricates the lymphatics and filters out the pathogens you bring into your body with the food you eat.

Our bodies need natural fats—butter, cream, and animal fats to keep the lymphatic system running strong.

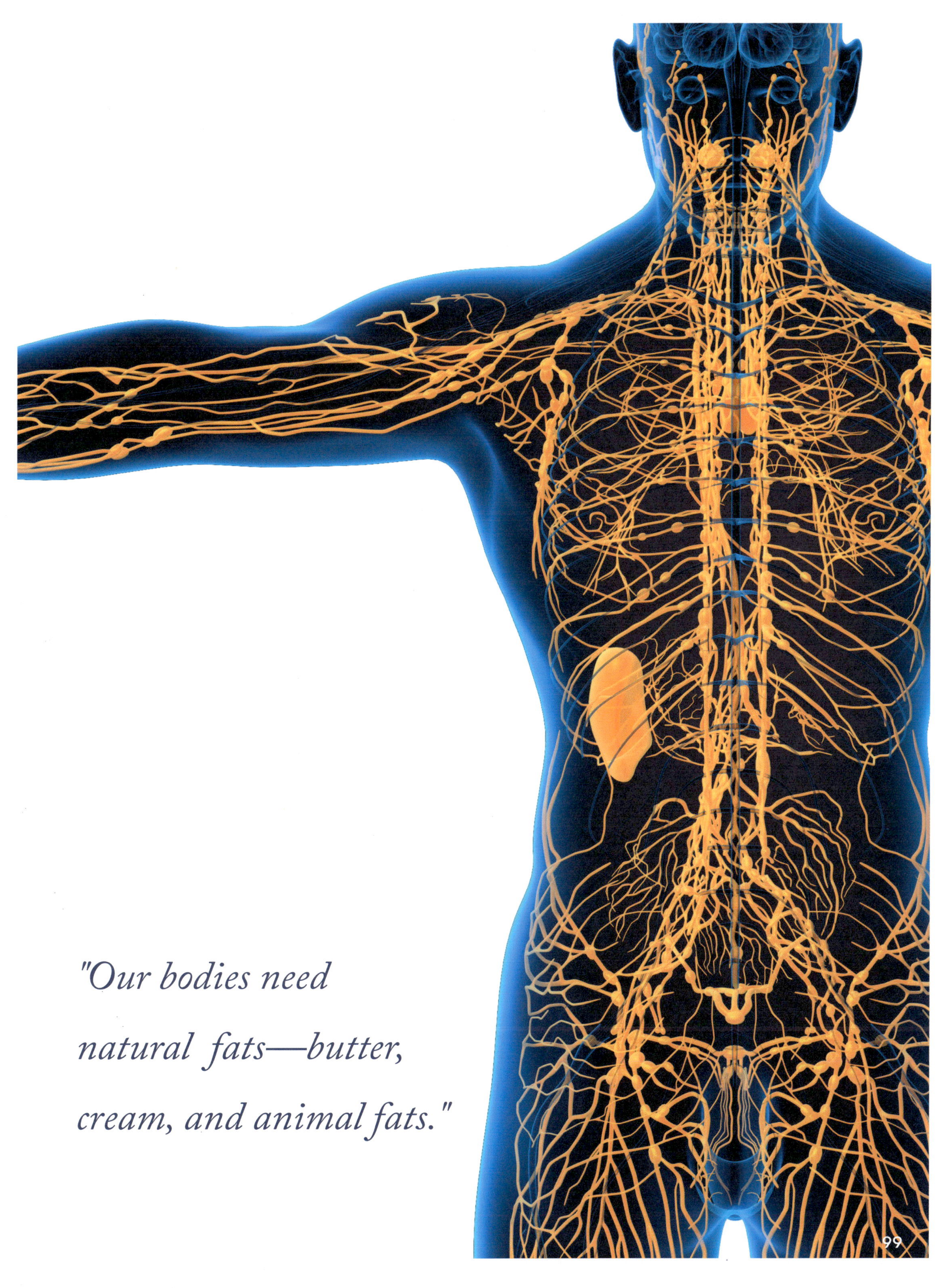

"Our bodies need natural fats—butter, cream, and animal fats."

Digestion 101

PROPER DIGESTION AND GUT HEALTH ARE CRITICAL TO YOUR HEALTH & WELLNESS

Over 2,000 years ago Hippocrates said, **"All disease begins in the gut."** He also declared **"Let food be thy medicine and medicine be thy food."** I see great truth in both statements. Scientists are starting to find hard ev=idence that what we eat has a profound effect upon our overall health—both mentally and physically. I've witnessed it personally in myself. Anything good or bad that is happening in the gut creates a domino effect throughout the body, and that includes the mind.

The digestive tract is an amazing machine that allows us to take in complex foods, plant material, animal material, and pretty much any material and break it down into the simple components of simple sugars, amino acids, and fatty acids.

Digestion involves many different organs, and the process begins even before we put anything into our mouths with our salivary glands that are activated by the sight or smell of food and begin to secrete saliva.

Food is manually broken down by our teeth and coated in saliva, which contains enzymes required for carbohydrate digestion.

The mechanical breakdown of food continues in the stomach where it is mixed with gastric juices and transformed into an acidic paste called chyme.

The small intestine then has a dual role as both a digestive organ and gland. The acidic pH of the chyme stimulates the production of messenger hormones that signal the pancreas and gallbladder. The pancreas is signaled to release bicarbonate (i.e., baking soda) to neutralize the chyme and pancreatic juice to help with digestion into the small intestine. The gallbladder is signaled to release bile, which emulsifies and absorbs fat into the lymphatics.

Our bodies take the carbon particles from carbohydrates, break them down in the gut, and takes the micronized carbon particles that have been broken down from complex sugars to simple sugars and passes them in to the hepatic portal system where they're shuttled off to the liver. In the liver, the sugars are converted to fat via insulin.

Proteins are broken down by enzymes into amino acids and absorbed into the hepatic portal blood flow to the liver and via insulin, converted to sugar and then fats.

The large intestine recycles water, captures any lost nutrients that are still available (with the help of the bowel flora), converts the nutrients to Vitamins K/B1/B2/B12 and butyric acid (fatty acid), and forms and expels fecal waste.

From the day we are born until the day we die, our bowels are digesting food—mostly carbs. Always exposing our bowels and body to the digestion process and chemicals that feed our cells and nourish our body. Our bowels never get a chance to rest; they never get a chance to heal. They are always inflamed! This is the entry point for most damage and disease. Our digestive system effectively becomes a compost heap.

THE PROCESS OF DIGESTION:

- Creates heat and gas, alcohol and aldehydes (all damaging to the intestinal cells and beyond)
- Creates churning that causes damage to the sensitive epithelial cells via fibers abrasive effects on the interstitial cells.
- Is unrelenting (no rest), meaning damage and repair are continuous causing inflammation that is the leading cause of our digestive disorders and distant cellular damage
- Damages the Teflon coating of the bowels, called the glycocalyx, exposing the epithelial cells to invasion by microbes (bacteria, yeast, viruses) and subsequently transports these microbes to every cell/organ in the body!
- Damages the glycocalyx--mostly from the abrasive nature of food and digestion--the often toxic particles of food (mostly plants with their methods of protection from organisms that eat them --oxylates, phytates, glutens, and others.

The ability to make fat fast and burn it slow allows us to go days and weeks without food. We're a fat-making and fat-burning machine. We must convert all fuel (sugar and amino acids) in the liver to fat. Fat is made in the liver via insulin that comes directly from the pancreas. If you don't have a normally functioning pancreas and liver, you can't make fat. **If you don't eat fat or make fat, you die.**

But if you eat real fat in the form of butter fat, cream fat, or animal fat, it's able to be absorbed via the chylomicrons that are developed in the GI tract from the secretion of bile into the gut, which is then taken up into the thoracic duct, the lymphatics of the GI tract. **The fat helps absorb the dirt and the dust in the bowels, and likely bind the microorganisms in the gut and trap them in the chylomicrons,** deliver them to the lymphatics (the thoracic duct), which delivers them to the filter system of the body which are the lymph nodes.

This is the way we capture them in the gut to send them to the thoracic duct/lymphatics to cleanse the real fuel of the body which is fat and deposit it in the adipose tissue of the butt, the belly, the thighs, and the arms and many more internal storage sites. This is the fuel tank for the Ferrari which allows you to go days, weeks, and even months without consuming food.

Ultimately all foods are used toproduce Acetyl CoA, then fat, which is ultimately used to produce ATP. ATP (Adenosine triphosphate) in the mitochondria; which is the necessary source of energy for every cell in our bodies.

Digestion is a parasympathetic process, which means the body must be in a relaxed state in order for things to work properly. This is why **the parasympathetic process** is also referred to as the body's "rest and digest" mode, while the **sympathetic mode** is known as the body's "fight or flight" mode.

If you're exercising or stressed, the body de-prioritizes and begins to shut down aspects of digestion in order to provide blood flow to the muscles or other organs that require it more urgently. This is another reason I say, **"One meal at night, then rest and digest."**

THE GUT

- 70-80% of our immune system resides in the gut. Good gut health is necessary for a healthy immune system.
- If digestion is impaired, our bodies can't absorb nutrients properly (leaky gut).
- Chronic digestive issues create chronic inflammation and stress, which can wreak havoc on the body and lead to cellular/organ/hormonal imbalances and disease.

BODY FAT STORAGE SITES

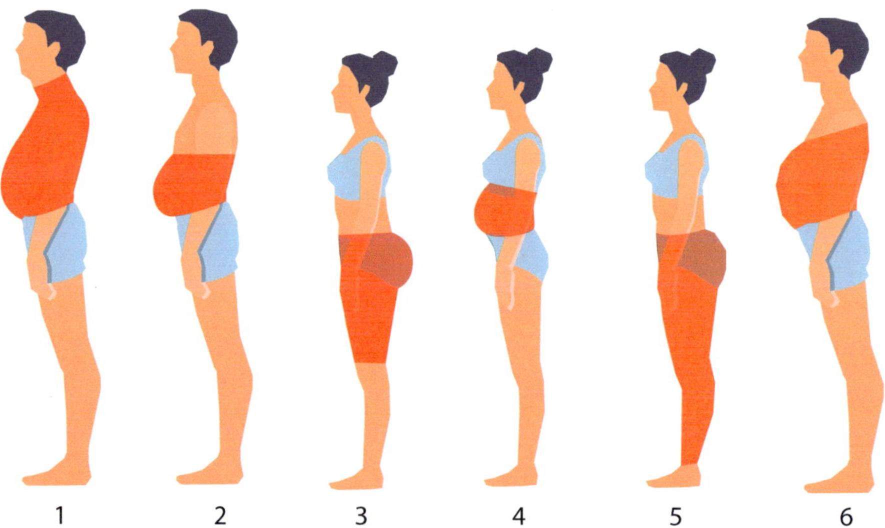

Stages of Digestion

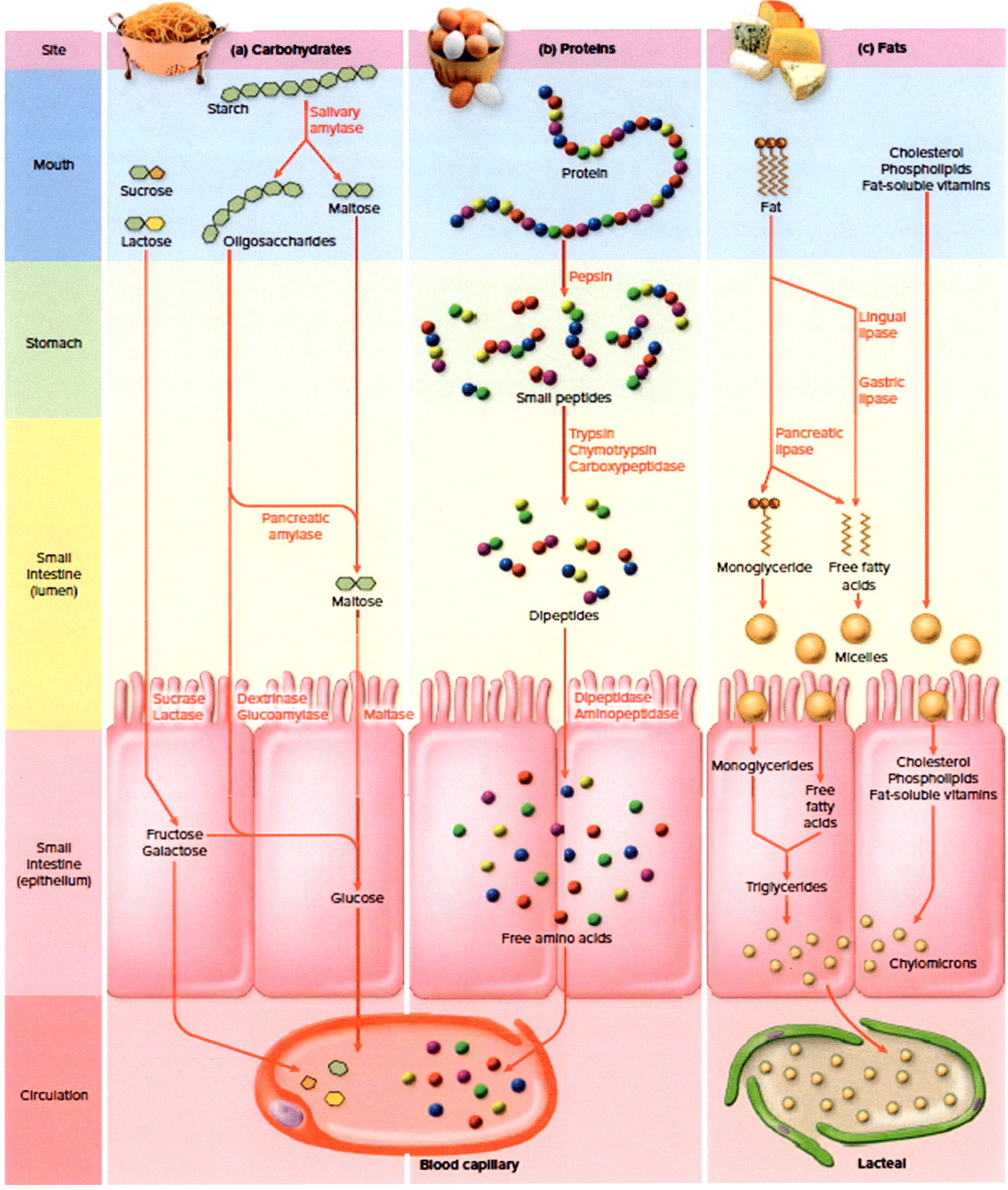

Intermittent Feasting:

TRUE FASTING: EAT ONCE PER DAY (OR LESS)

Fasting between meals gives your body time to rest and digest, heal and repair, and allows the glucose levels in the bloodstream and throughout the body to go down. Some refer to this as "intermittent fasting", but I find the term "intermittent feasting" to be more accurate. I believe your best health comes from eating one meal a day in the evening and giving the body time to clear the bowels of food by allowing 12-24 hours between feedings. This is in line with how prehistoric man lived: going for days to weeks without eating, not knowing where or when his next meal was coming, feasting and then fasting, fasting, fasting while on the hunt for food.

Our bodies were not designed to eat 3-5 meals a day with snacks in between like a grazing animal. Eating several meals a day fills the gut with fiber and carbs that ferment and feed the bacteria and yeast causing more disease. The more we eat, the more we fill **"the bucket"** that is our digestive system. We fuel the fire of inflammation; we fill our intestines, never allowing them to diminish their contents because of the continuous supply of food.

Intermittent feasting allows time for digestion, reduces glucose and insulin levels in the bloodstream, thereby reducing the damage that causes foggy brain, digestive issues, and aches and pains throughout the body.

Our bodies are well- designed to go without food, yet most of us consume more calories than we could ever burn through in a day. This adds fat to our bodies. Fat is meant to be there to help ensure our survival during times of famine and drought.

Dr. Jason Fung has a lot of good information on incorporating intermittent fasting into your lifestyle.

"Carbo-caine" When I talk to patients or friends about eating bacon, eggs, butter, and beef and removing carbohydrates and sugar from their diets, most worry they won't be able to do it. Carbs and sugar have a real grip on most of us, you're not imagining it. I actually call carbs "carbo-caine". Like cocaine, they are addictive. Eating carbs affects the pleasure centers in the brain just like a drug. High carb consumption spikes insulin which allows tryptophan to enter the brain and make serotonin, the feel-good neurotransmitter.

Eating carbs quite literally makes us happy, but only temporarily. A steady diet of high carbs and sugar will create a host of problems that affect your daily enjoyment of life and can shorten your lifespan.

LONGER FASTING LEADS TO MORE LASTING!

Intermittent Feasting Benefits

While there are likely dozens of health benefits to intermittent feasting, we'd like to highlight a few that are especially important for impacting fertility.

BENEFIT #1: Keeping the Bowels Clear and Cool

Many people do not recognize that in the female body, the bowels sit directly on top of the reproductive organs.

This is problematic as digestion (particularly fermentation if you are eating vegetable products) creates a tremendous amount of heat, and the female reproductive system is fine-tuned to function at a very specific temperature, 98.6.

This isn't a problem if we space out meals and limit them to around once a day. But if we are eating 3 meals a day and snacking in between, the ovaries may be operating in elevated temperatures nearly 24/7, which could seriously alter egg quality and other aspects of female reproductive health.

BENEFIT #2: Increases Human Growth Hormone -> Improves Egg & Sperm Quality

We frequently prescribe human growth hormone or recommend supplements designed to increase HGH levels as a way of improving egg quality. But all of that may not be necessary if you're intermittently feasting.

A recent study looking at the effects of IF on 200 people found that fasting for just a 24-hour period increased HGH by 1300% in women and 2000% in men.

BENEFIT #3: Reduces Inflammation

Fasting has been shown in numerous studies to reduce inflammatory activities and reduce chronic inflammation. This gives IF the power to improve nearly every marker of physical and mental health while reducing the risk of disease and infertility.

BENEFIT #4: Improved Blood Sugar, Insulin, and Hormone Levels

It is believed that PCOS, a leading cause of infertility, is largely driven and caused by chronically elevated blood glucose levels which keep insulin levels consistently high and lead to disruption of normal hormone function.

Fasting is the most foolproof way to reduce blood glucose and insulin levels, and reduce the symptoms of metabolic syndrome and PCOS, including ovulatory dysfunction.

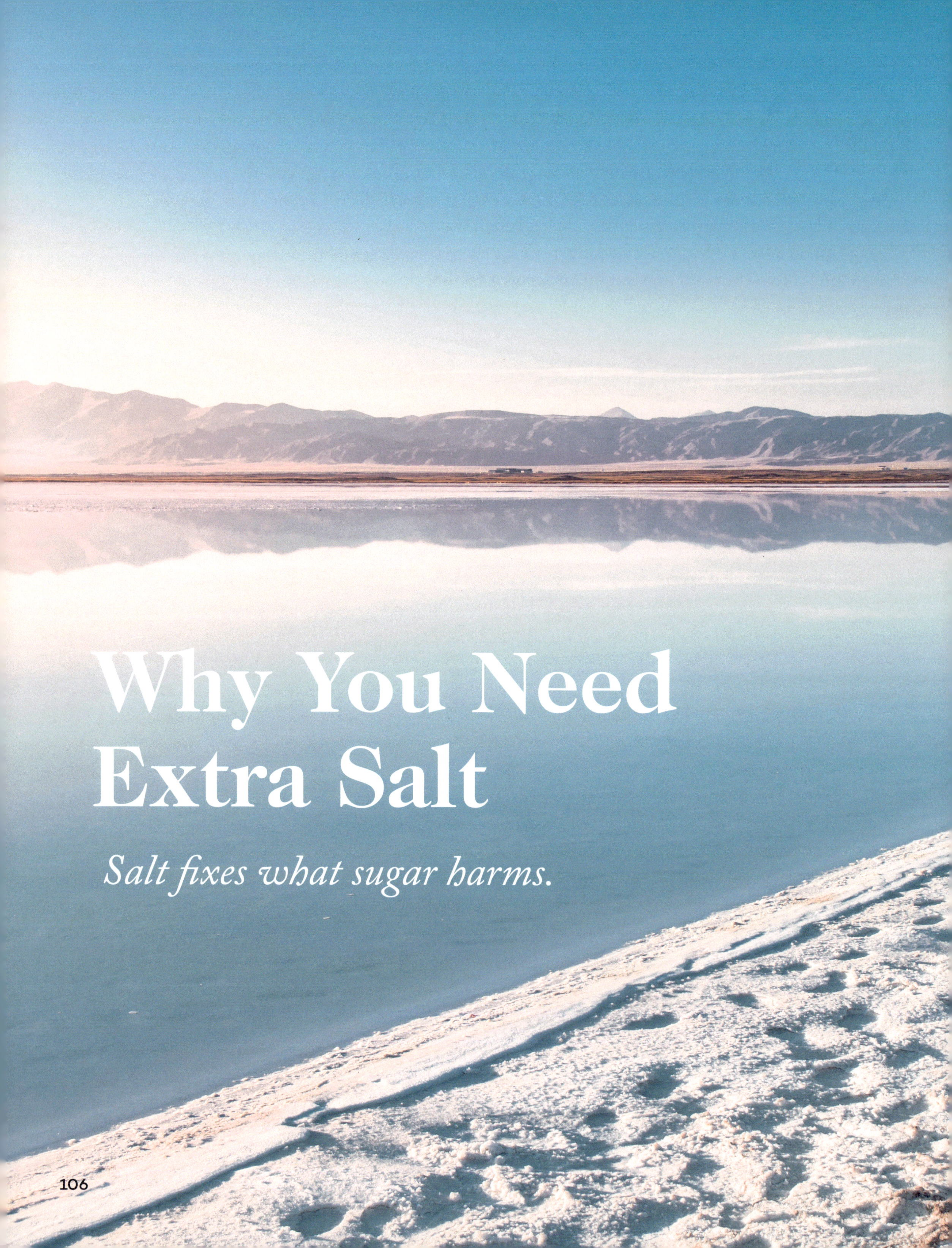

Why You Need Extra Salt

Salt fixes what sugar harms.

In Dr. Kiltz's B.E.B.B.I.S. Diet (Bacon, Eggs, Butter, Beef, Ice Cream, Salt), salt is a critical component. Your body uses salt to help regulate fluid balance. As you're eating fewer processed foods and your body begins to sheds electrolytes and fluids while in ketosis, your body also loses salt. Even transitioning from regular keto to the B.E.B.B.I.S. Diet, you will lose extra water from inflammation.

How do you know you need more salt? Feeling foggy (brain fog) or lethargic, muscle cramps/spasms, headache/dehydration/hungover, dizziness going from sitting to standing are all likely symptoms. The solution is usually more salt. If you add a little more sea salt to your diet and you feel better, then that's your answer. Often salting your food to taste isn't enough to compensate for the volume of salt you've lost. When more salt doesn't do the trick, you may need to try adding potassium or magnesium. **Soaking in an Epsom Salt bath can also help as you absorb salt's active ingredients** magnesium and sulfate through your skin.

Like red meat, salt has been demonized, but that other white crystalline substance **(SUGAR) is a much bigger threat than salt ever was!** New studies are showing that salt may not be as damaging to health as previously claimed. There's growing evidence to suggest that a moderate intake of sodium may have a beneficial role in cardiovascular health, but a potentially more harmful role when intake is very high or very low.

For those who want to go dairy-free, but have difficulty kicking the dairy habit, salt is sometimes one of the problems. There are lots of salty cheeses. If your body is craving salt, it can make removing dairy products more challenging.

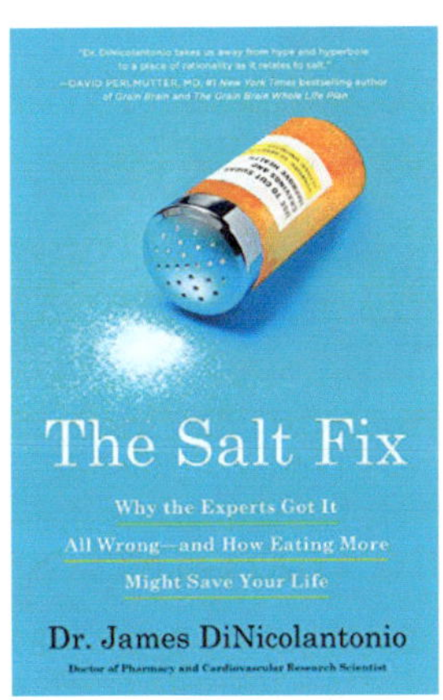

*Check Out **The Salt Fix** by Dr. James DiNicolantonio*

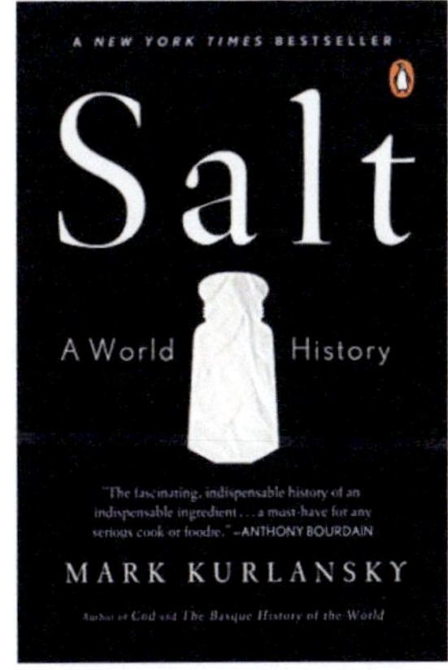

*Check Out **Salt: A World History** by Mark Kurlansky*

How Do I Get Started?

It's helpful to "buddy up" when starting Keto. Adopting the Carnivore lifestyle with a partner or friend allows you to share, learn from and support each other. Many of our client couples go Keto together and find they are both happier and healthier. When it comes to fertility, both the man's and woman's health are important and play a role in conception.

And you don't have to go 100% Carnivore cold turkey.
It's okay to take baby-steps and gradually incorporate the Carnivore lifestyle into your everyday living. Start by decreasing your carb intake and cutting out sugar. Consider eliminating all processed foods from your diet. If it comes in a bag or a box, it's processed. A good pantry and refrigerator clean-out can help reduce temptation. Donate unopened boxes and bags to your local food pantry. Then re-stock your refrigerator with real food, the way nature made it: fatty meats, poultry, and seafoods. Avoid foods with preservatives and coloring, both of which can be detrimental to our health.

Buy organic when possible and grass-fed beef. Farmers markets are a great place to find locally grown/raised foods.

And don't expect to be perfect. None of us is. You will have days when you don't stick to your goals and you make bad food choices—you have a glass of wine with a friend or eat a couple French fries. That's okay. Just get back on track and stay focused.

The good news is that a carnivore diet is generally more fulfilling than one heavy in carbs and sugar.

Fats are filling. Even though you are eating less, you will feel fuller faster and not get hungry as fast because your sugar levels aren't on a roller coaster anymore.

GETTING STARTED ON DR. KILTZ'S CARNIVORE

1. **Get rid of all sugar—**

   Any type.
2. **Get rid of all grains —**

   wheat, corn, rice, oats.
3. **Get rid of all hydrogenated or partially hydrogenated oils (e.g. vegetables oils)**—canola oil, grapeseed oil, corn or sunflower oil, and most vegetable oils contain Polyunsaturated fatty acids (PUFAs) and are very inflammatory. These should be eliminated (or kept to a minimum like peanut or sesame oil).
4. **Get rid of all fruits, vegetables, and fiber.**
5. **Practice intermittent feasting.** Narrow your eating window to 1-2 hours per day with 1 meal and 1-2 snacks.

Carnivore is for everyone.

TIPS for Keeping Carnivore on a Budget

CHEAP MEATS - BETTER THAN EXPENSIVE PLANTS

Interested in getting started with the carnivore diet, but worried about the cost of all that meat? You'll be happy to learn that it's possible to go carnivore without breaking the bank. Here are some tips and strategies for eating carnivore on a budget.

1. Try organ meats, ground beef, eggs, and other underrated foods
2. Use tallow and suet for cooking
3. Go for cheaper, fattier meats
4. Buy bone-in cuts which generally cost less
5. Eat only one or two meals a day
6. Shop around and/or buy a cow share

Budget-Friendly Carnivore Foods

1. Ground Beef
2. Sardines
3. Atlantic Mackerel
4. Eggs
5. Beef Tallow
6. Pork Belly
7. Cream Cheese

Organ Meats

A well-formulated carnivore plan doesn't mean eating only the most popular cuts of steak like ribeye and filet mignon. Fortunately, organ meats are among nature's most underrated superfoods and some of the cheapest foods available. Many grocery stores and butcher shops sell beef liver and other organs for $1-2 per pound. Even organic, grass-fed beef liver is relatively affordable compared to muscle meat.

If you've tried liver, experienced its impressive benefits and are curious about other organ meat, here are a few more budget-friendly options:

- Beef Liver
- Beef Kidney
- Sweetbreads
- Bone Marrow
- Spleen
- Brain
- Tripe

Muscle Meat

Muscle meat, also known as skeletal muscle, is the meat of animals that's found in the muscles. It includes ground meats, but also some less obvious options like gizzards, hearts, cheeks, and tongue.

RATIO OF FAT TO PROTEIN

1:1	2:1	3:1
Ok	**Good**	**Great**

Eggs

Eggs may be the cheapest whole-animal food out there. An egg contains every nutrient needed to produce a future chicken. Eggs are rich in several nutrients that beef is lacking, including vitamin K2 and vitamin E. Just like beef liver, even high-quality eggs are pretty affordable.

Tallow and Suet

A well-formulated carnivore plan doesn't mean Lard and tallow are two of the most carnivore-friendly cooking fats. They're also two of the cheapest. Both fats go for just $1-2 per pound — less if you befriend your local butcher--making them one of the cheapest foods per calorie. Lard and beef tallow are also incredibly satiating. Eating these fats can help you in cutting back on other foods, saving you more money.

As an added benefit, the stearic saturated fatty acids in tallow are great for your health. Research shows that their intake promotes mitochondrial fission, a process where mitochondria orient themselves towards burning visceral fat for fuel.

Buy Cheaper, Fattier Cuts of Meat

Cheap Cuts	Moderate Cuts	Expensive cuts
Ground beef Chuck roast Stew meat	Top Round Bottom Round Eye of Round Skirt Steak	Ribeye T-Bone New York Strip Filet Mignon Flank Steak

Low-fat misinformation has caused many people to seek leaner cuts of meat. The upside to this faulty diet dogma means that fattier cuts of meat are often surprisingly cheap. Therefore, you can save additional money by choosing lower grades of beef.

Contrary to conventional wisdom, lower-grade beef isn't necessarily less safe or even lower quality. The USDA's grading system is based on the marbling, tenderness, and flavor of any given cut. Even the chewiest piece of beef can become melt-in-your-mouth tender if it's cooked right (low and slow is the way to go).

- Cheapest option: Select grade
- Moderate option: Choice grade
- Priciest option: Prime grade

Opt for Bone-in Cuts

Bone-in beef is almost always cheaper than boneless, even when you factor in the weight of the bones you're not able to eat. And these marrow bones are nutritiously valuable when it comes to making homemade bone broth.

Shop Around or Buy a Cow Share

It pays to buy in bulk for most items, and carnivore-friendly foods are no exception. Apps like Instacart are great for searching bulk deals, allowing you to compare prices of similar items across different stores.

Below are several more places to find volume deals:

- Costco
- Local farms
- Your local butcher

Many farms and butcher shops allow you to buy anywhere from a quarter-cow to a whole cow at a time, often for a steep discount. Once acquired, you can then piece your cow, store in a chest freezer, and thaw what you need each week. Whole cows can be expensive up-front, but some people find a workaround by combining their buying power with like-minded family or friends.

OMAD + 1-2 Snacks

Perhaps the simplest way to do the carnivore diet on a budget is to eat less often.

By incorporating intermittent fasting (or feasting, as I like to say) and eating one carnivorous meal a day, you'll be able to stay satiated while saving on your grocery bill. The high fat and protein content of a carnivore diet is so satiating that many people fall into this type of meal frequency naturally.

Adding Liver to Your Diet

Liver is one of the most nutrient-dense foods on earth. Prized by our ancestors for millennia, liver is making a comeback thanks to nose-to-tail aficionados.

Despite its health benefits, not everyone finds liver particularly delicious. Try transforming your beef liver into any of the following dishes if you're trying to give it a taste an upgrade:

Make A Smooth and Salty Pate

"Pâté" is the French word for 'paste' and includes a mix of meat, veggies, spices, or even seafood. Some pates are super smooth, while others are chunkier. French cuisine has used pates to mask or enhance the taste of organ meats for centuries. Most people who try pate find it surprisingly tasty.

To make pate, simply blend cooked beef liver, onions, chives, and the spices of your choice in a food processor. Once it's been mixed, place your pate in the refrigerator in a sealed container and serve chilled.

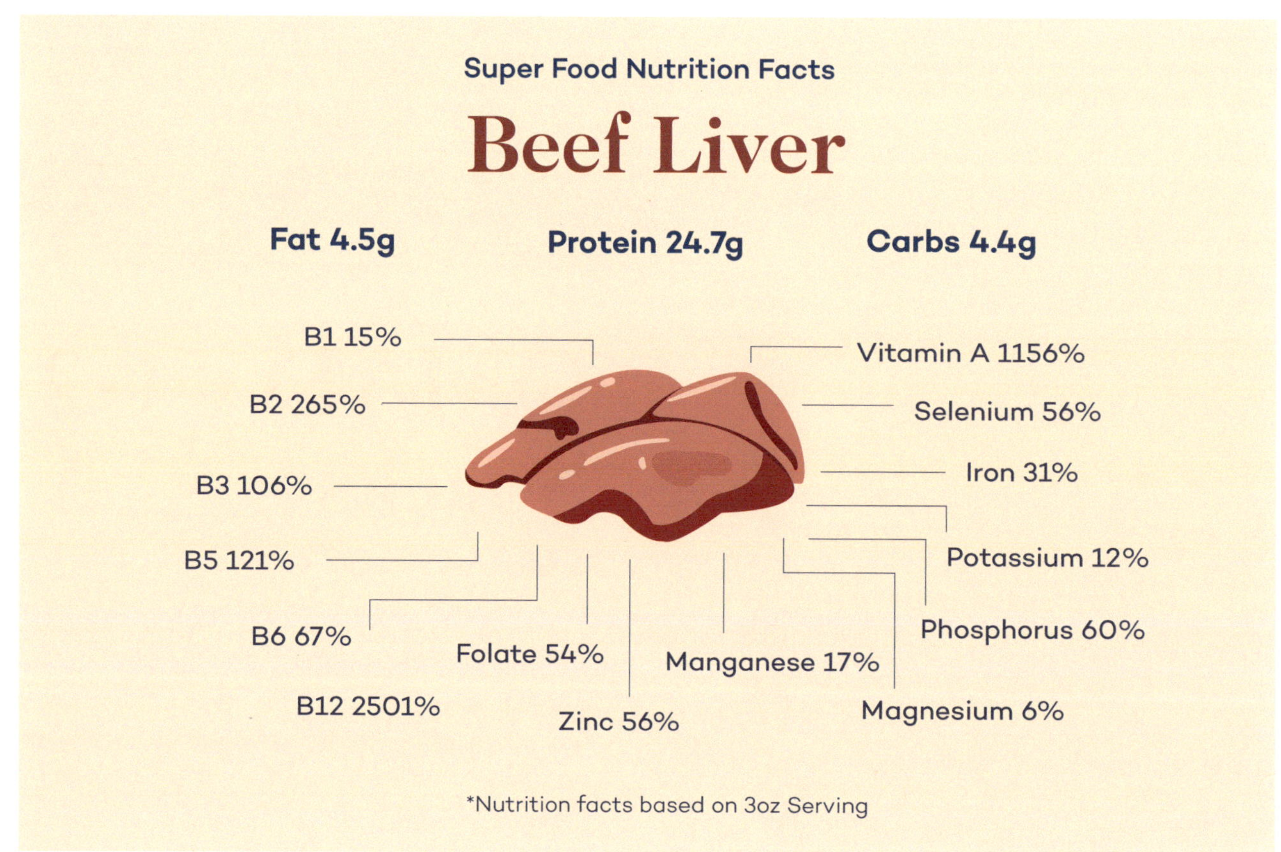

Benefits of Eating Liver

Why eat beef liver?

Because it contains a robust blend of nutrients found nowhere else in nature:

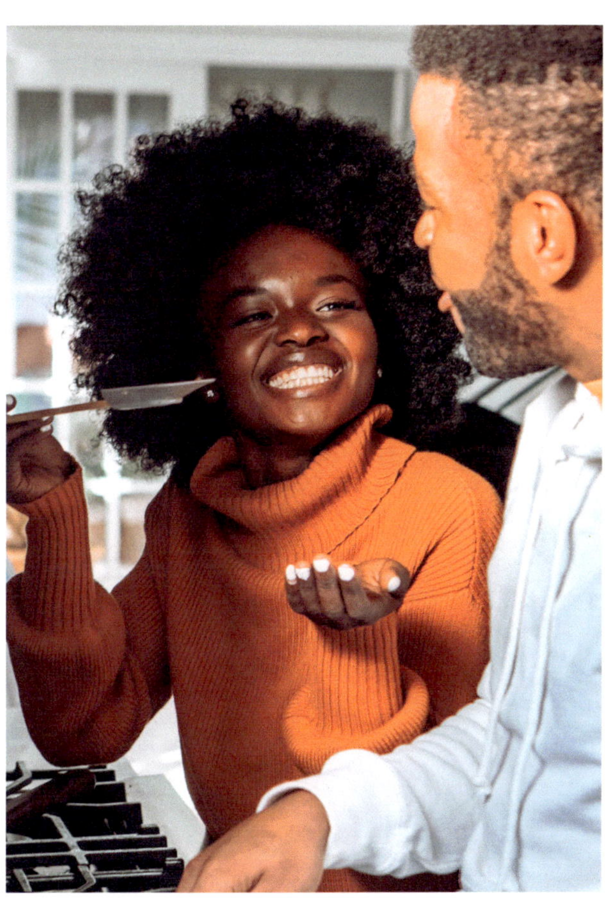

1. **VITAMIN B12** assists with red blood cell production. It also plays a vital role in brain cell metabolism.

2. **COPPER** works with zinc to activate the immune system. It also activates important enzymes to regulate cellular energy production.

3. **VITAMIN A** is critical when it comes to maintaining vision, immunity, and skin health. It also helps your body's own liver and other organs function correctly.

4. **RIBOFLAVIN/B2** is one of the most pro-metabolic B vitamins—it helps convert the food you eat into usable energy.

5. **CHOLINE** is a B vitamin that's especially important when it comes to cognitive development and liver health.

6. **FOLATE/B9** is yet another pro-metabolic B vitamin that assists with cell growth and differentiation. It's of utmost importance for women who are pregnant or hoping to become pregnant.

7. **IRON** is an essential nutrient that distributes oxygen throughout your body. The iron in beef liver takes the form of highly bioavailable heme iron.

Mix it with other Meats

Liver usually comes in whole pieces, but you might consider asking your butcher about ground liver — it's much easier to work with and incorporate into other dishes. **Once you've got a package of ground liver, you can mix it 20/80 with regular ground beef.** Chances are you won't even notice the liver. If anything, the mixture will taste slightly sweeter than your normal ground beef. It can be made into hamburgers, cheeseburgers, meatballs, and meatloaf.

Bathe it in Tallow or Butter

When in doubt, there's a classic way to enjoy beef liver: **fry it in liberal amounts of salt and butter.** This approach is both simple and effective. First, place a pan over high heat, then melt some butter or tallow in the pan. Once the cooking fat is nice and hot, add some thin strips of liver. Finish by adding some salt and bacon for extra crunch and flavor.

Eat it Raw

Yep, you read that right. **Beef liver can indeed be enjoyed raw.** Dr. Kiltz likes to get the liver, slice it down, and freeze it flat. Then he takes out a small piece at a time, cuts it into swallowable, bite-size pieces, salts it, lets it defrost a few minutes. Then he takes a tiny chew with water and down it goes.

Many raw liver fans find that it has a sweet flavor and pleasant mouthfeel, though some of the more nuanced aspects of liver's taste are lost during cooking. Just be aware that raw liver is pretty chewy, so be sure to slice it into thin pieces or small cubes before enjoying it.

The age of the liver you're preparing also contributes to its flavor. Veal liver has a milder taste, while mature animal liver may taste stronger and earthier.

Other ideas for preparing liver

- **Pan-fry liver,** onions, and mushrooms with some butter
- **Chop some liver,** then mix with regular ground beef into meatballs and serve with tomato sauce
- **Use calf or lamb liver** instead of mature beef liver for a milder taste
- **Soak your liver in milk** or lemon before cooking to reduce its flavor

Remember that quality matters when it comes to beef liver's benefits. Source your liver from New Zealand if you don't have access to organic cattle farms you can trust. And, regardless of what you do with liver, be sure to enjoy your journey towards better health!

Carnivore Snacks

Interested in getting started with the carnivore diet, but worried about the cost of all that meat? You'll be happy to learn that it's possible to go carnivore without breaking the bank. Here are some tips and strategies for eating carnivore on a budget.

Top Whole Food Carnivore Snacks

Steak Leftovers

Eggs

Cheese

Butter

Pork Rinds

Freeze Dried Beef Organs

Beef Jerky & Biltong

Kiltz Ice Cream (No Sugar)

Bone Broth

High quality preserved meats:

Prosciutto, Speck, Serrano Ham, Salamis, etc.

Bone Broth: Why You Should Be Drinking It Too

Have you seen the term "bone broth" popping up on carnivore blogs and recipes? You may have seen it on the shelves of your local grocery store or Trader Joe's and wondered what it was. So, what is it and why should you be jumping on the bandwagon?

Bone broth is exactly what its name implies. **It's a broth made from cooking down animal bones and other connective tissue** (feet, beaks, spines, gizzard, legs, hooves, hocks, or even the whole carcass) with water and adding an acid like vinegar or lemon juice to help break down the collagen. It can be made from chicken, turkey, lamb, pig, beef, fish, and other wild game. Many people roast the bones first for a richer, deeper flavored broth.

Bones contain lots of nutrients which provide some pretty impressive health benefits. It's high in various minerals, collagen, glycine, glucosamine and chondroitin.

BONE: The bone itself yields minerals like calcium and phosphorus. Sodium, magnesium, potassium, sulfur and silicon are also present.

MARROW: Bone marrow gives you vitamin A, vitamin K2, omega-3s, omega-6s and minerals like iron, zinc, selenium, boron and manganese. Marrow from beef and lamb also contains CLA.

CONNECTIVE TISSUE: This tissue provides glucosamine and chondroitin, which are popular dietary supplements for arthritis and joint pain.

While it can be used as an ingredient in soups and sauces, many people drink a cup as part of their regular daily routine. It's a great snack and a soothing way to start or end the day. Adding a bit of extra sea salt to your bone broth and drinking it in the early stages of transitioning to carnivore can help ward off the keto flu. When you stop eating so many processed foods, you take in a lot less sodium, some of which your body needs. This is one way to add it back.

POTENTIAL HEALTH BENEFITS INCLUDE:

- **Anti-inflammatory:** The glycine may have some anti-inflammatory and antioxidant effects.
- **Weight Loss:** It's low in calories and sugar-free, but still helps you feel full. This may be due to its gelatin content, which can promote satiety.
- **Joint Health:** Glucosamine and chondroitin improve joint health and reduce symptoms of osteoarthritis.
- **Bone Health:** Calcium, magnesium and phosphorus all promote good bone health.
- **Sleep and Brain Function:** Glycine taken before bed has been shown to improve sleep and brain function.

Whether you buy it or make it, **the health and flavor of the bone broth is ultimately dependent on the quality of the ingredients:** where did the bones come from? What did the animals eat? How long was it cooked? If you don't have the time to make it yourself, be sure to read the ingredients of various bone broths before you settle on one to try. Kettle & Fire makes a good one, but there are other quality bone broths out there.

If you make it right, you'll see bits of "jelly" in your broth. Bones, marrow and connective tissue are all largely made up of collagen, which turns into gelatin when cooked.

Simple Bone Broth Recipe

INGREDIENTS

- 2–3 pounds of beef bones.
- 4 liters (1 gallon) of water.
- 2 tablespoons apple cider vinegar.
- 1 onion (optional).
- 4 garlic cloves (optional).
- 1 teaspoon of salt and/or pepper (optional).

DIRECTIONS

Put bones and vegetables in a big, stainless steel pot*.

Pour cold water into the pot so it covers the contents. Add the vinegar, and then raise the temperature to bring to a boil.

Reduce heat, add salt and pepper, and then let simmer for 4–24 hours (the longer it simmers, the tastier and more nutrient-dense it will be).

Allow the broth to cool, and then strain the solids out.

Now it's ready.

You can also add other meat, veggies or spices to your broth. Popular additions include parsley, bay leaves, carrots, celery, ginger, lemon rinds and liver, but they are not required.

Broth may be stored in an airtight container in the refrigerator for up to 5 days, or in the freezer for up to 3 months.

For those who prefer to multi-task (cook and sleep), you may also want to use a pressure cooker, slow cooker or Crock-Pot. You can use a Crock-Pot to make bone broth overnight.

***For extra flavor, roast the bones before adding to pot. Preheat oven to 450°. Roast bones on a parchment-lined rimmed baking sheet for 30 minutes.**

Carnivore Journeys

Karin W.

Carnivore for 4 years

What's your story?

I was 47 years old and had been in constant pain 24 hours a day in almost all my muscles, tendons, ligaments, haircuts, bursae in the neck, shoulders, arms, hands, hips, legs, knees and feet, since September 2014. I was exhausted from the pain...

The doctors gave me painkillers, rheumatism medication and stomach protectors. Because of the stomach protectors, my body was unable to absorb vitamins from my diet more and more, so I started to feel worse. Work was no longer possible. I couldn't do anything anymore, but the doctors said: "You'll just have to learn to live with it..." **How then?**

A physiotherapist gave me the tip to look at my diet and advised me to read the book "The food hourglass" Slowly I started to eliminate food. I started cutting out sugar. Paleo, Low Carb, Keto and now Carnivore. I have been completely pain-free for a few years now, better mental health, no more depression/suicidal thoughts, no more constipation, more energy and 30 kg lighter!

In addition to eating carnivore, I also fast. 21 hours of no food and 3 hours of eating. And drink bulk. Drink more than a liter of water twice a day. Self-knowledge: I now know that I can and continue to function without food for a while.

Tips for others starting the carnivore journey:

Start slowly. For at least 3 months. Don't give up when it gets hard.

Agnieszka and Michal Kaca

Carnivore for 6 weeks

How are you feeling?

More energy, no cravings! Lots of positives:)

What's your story?

Dr. Kiltz has inspired me to try Keto Carnivore. It was sooo HARD at the beginning. Making meals that are keto carnivore , no carbs. My husband has decided to try Keto Carnivore too and he like the effects! We cheat on the weekends but the carbs don't taste sooo addictive like they used to.

Tips for others starting the carnivore journey:

Don't give up! It's only tough for a first week or two, then it gets only better and easier :)

Jeff Benjamin

Keto for 13 months

What are you eating?

2MAD:

Lunch @ noon: 8 oz wild caught salmon, 4 oz brocollini

Dinner: 10 oz chicken breast breaded with pork rinds ground, 4 oz hard raw goat milk cheddar cheese, pork rinds, 4 oz Lillys sugar free 85% dark chocolate

What results are you seeing?

T2D reversed: started at A1c of 11.2, now 5.2

Lost 125 lbs

Shirt size from 3x to L, pant waist size from 54 to 33

Describe your journey

Thankful for my T2 diabetes diagnosis. Really. There is nothing else which could have gotten me to be healthier than ever, and gotten me to be confident I will remain as healthy as possible.

Because of T2, I:

- Monitor my health every day
- Know everything I put in my body, and why
- Take control over one of the few things I can in this life
- Have confidence that I do all I can for my health
- Changed my lifestyle, instead of dieting
- Stopped eating poison (aka the standard American diet)
- Can help others if they want it

Without this diagnosis, I am sure I would have continued with undiagnosed hyperinsulinemia and died of cardio-vascular disease.

And because I've reversed my T2 (A1C of 11.2 to 5.2), I can confidently ignore advice some (most?) "experts" give to those with this disease because I am living proof that doing it the right way (very low carb, whole real food) works. It's right there in my bloodwork results.

This lifestyle saved me. My T2 diagnosis has made me better. For scared newcomers to this group, you can choose to embrace your diagnosis to make yourself healthier and better than ever.

Tips for others:

Give it time. It took a very long time to get to the state you are in. Healing that will take some time. Trust that the human body is built to heal itself of most conditions if you fuel it properly.

Craig R.

Carnivore for 13 months

What are you eating?

Lunch - ground beef, bacon and eggs

Dinner - a ribeye or chuckeye and some oysters

How are you feeling?

"No more allergy attacks. No more asthma/breathing issues. No more canker sores."

No more soreness after working out and can do so much more. Doing about 150-250 pushups a day. Doing about 150-250 crunches a day. I don't poop 6-8 times a day. I weigh less than I did in high school and no more protruding belly. **I have more confidence."**

Tips for others starting the carnivore journey:

"Give it at least 60 days to see how you feel. May want to ease into it by cutting one thing a week for a few weeks. Do not be afraid of salt and fat and cholesterol numbers."

Root Cause Healing with the Carnivore Diet

By Austin Cavelli, MS, PA-C

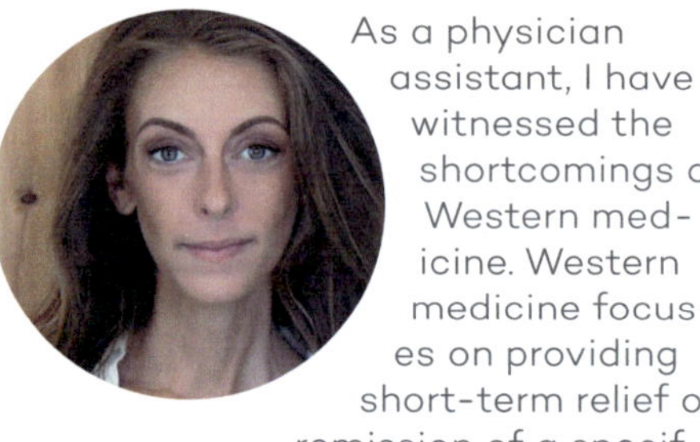

As a physician assistant, I have witnessed the shortcomings of Western medicine. Western medicine focuses on providing short-term relief or remission of a specific symptom, typically physical, like pain, and often by way of medications and/or surgery. This is a band-aid or quick-fix approach that does not address the underlying problem, namely inflammation. Root cause healing, instead, focuses on permanent healing, addressing the source of the inflammation throughout the body, on a deeper and larger scale. Bio-individuality, or uniqueness, is also critical and is often disregarded in Western medicine. Every individual is unique and should be treated as such. What a person does consistently each day matters and the diet must be at the forefront in changing one's health.

Biochemically, you are what you eat and absorb. A proper diet provides nutrients for fuel and support of every structure of the body down to the cellular level. The carnivore diet is comprised of the most nutrient dense foods on the planet, animal products. **Animal products provide the most "bang for your buck"** in terms of nutrients per calorie. The diet also eliminates all plants, as these contain anti-nutrients. Antinutrients are chemicals made by plants as a protective mechanism that bind to and prevent our body's ability to absorb vitamins and minerals. By eating only animal products, the body is being healed on a biochemical level by maximizing the amount of nutrients received while, at the same time, eliminating the intake of anti-nutrients. Even more, multiple nutrients are not available from plant sources including essential amino acids like creatine, carnosine, and taurine along with sufficient levels of B12.

Plant anti-nutrients also significantly compromise the gut lining, further impacting nutrient absorption. An impaired gut cannot properly absorb nutrients. Many Americans suffer from leaky gut syndrome without even knowing due to years of consumption of grains, sugar, seed and vegetable oils, plants and trending high fiber, high carbohydrate, low fat diets. This is a leading cause of many chronic diseases. The proportion of a nutrient that is actually digested, absorbed, and metabolized by the body is referred to as the bioavailability of nutrients. Bioavailability is highest and most efficient from animal food sources as compared to plants. The carnivore way of eating therefore allows the gut to heal and, in turn, improves nutrient absorption.

HEALING THE GUT IS ESSENTIAL TO HEAL THE BRAIN.

There is a direct connection between the gut and the brain, known as the gut-brain axis. With healing of the gut, the carnivore diet also provides healing of the brain including improvements in mood disorders like anxiety and depression, as well as improved mental clarity and focus. And it doesn't stop there.

The array of symptoms that are resolved with this way of eating spans all organ systems. This further indicates that underlying dysregulation and inflammation is being addressed; root cause healing is occurring throughout the body with this diet.
For these reasons, a carnivore diet is often utilized as an elimination approach for individuals struggling with multiple vague symptoms. A time frame for this approach has not been established, however I personally recommend at least a 3 month commitment for those looking to initiate root cause healing.

If clients are struggling to feel better or see significant improvements in symptoms with a carnivore approach, it is most commonly related to not eating appropriate amounts of fat. **Adequate fat in combination with the elimination of carbohydrates is what makes the carnivore diet unique.** It is a zero carb, high fat approach that puts the body into a state of ketosis to reduce overall inflammation and utilize fat as its main energy source. Fat is essential for root cause healing, to regulate hormones and improve brain function among many other processes. Fat is also necessary for absorption of the essential nutrients including fat soluble vitamins A, D, E, & K.

There is significant anecdotal evidence supporting a carnivore diet for multiple diagnoses because it truly allows for root cause healing throughout the body. Reversal of disease has been demonstrated in people with various autoimmune conditions, cancer, diabetes, and cardiovascular disease, just to name a few. But this elimination approach can also provide significant healing in those without symptoms or a medical diagnosis. After a 3 month experimentation period, I have witnessed the impact this diet has to create a level of health that far surpasses what an individual thought was their best. These individuals develop a new baseline level of what "feeling good" means. They experience a new "normal" that they didn't realize existed. Root cause healing is possible with a carnivore diet as it provides maximization of nutrients, gutbrain healing, improved nutrient absorption, and an anti-inflammatory effect throughout the body by relying on fat for fuel. These are the pillars of optimal health. Make it a lifestyle by adding in daily sun, movement, quality sleep, stress-management, and community and long-term health and longevity can be achieved.

Root cause healing is possible with a carnivore diet as it provides maximization of nutrients, gutbrain healing, improved nutrient absorption, and an anti-inflammatory effect throughout the body by relying on fat for fuel.

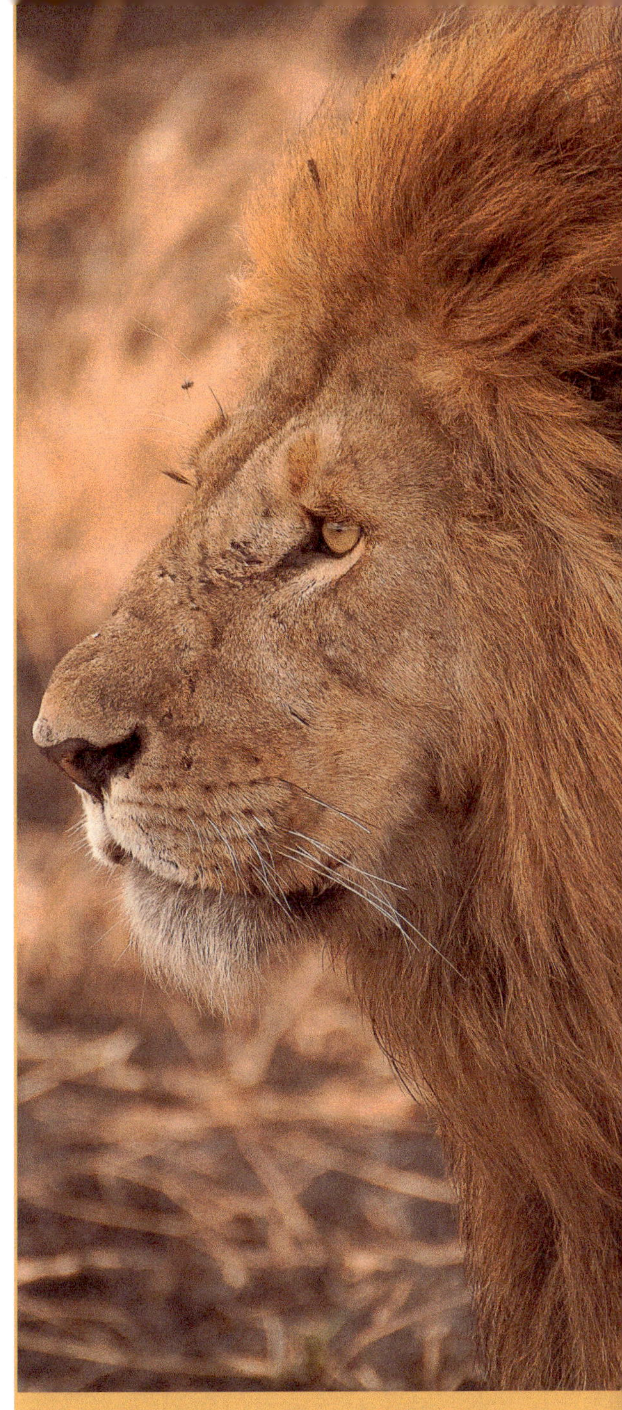

Austin is a Physician Assistant & Dietary Consultant and a Ketogenic & Carnivore Lifestyle Specialist who helps people optimize their health by burning fat for fuel and reducing years of underlying inflammation from the standard American diet. Her approach focuses on quality nutrition by way of nutrient-dense animal products.

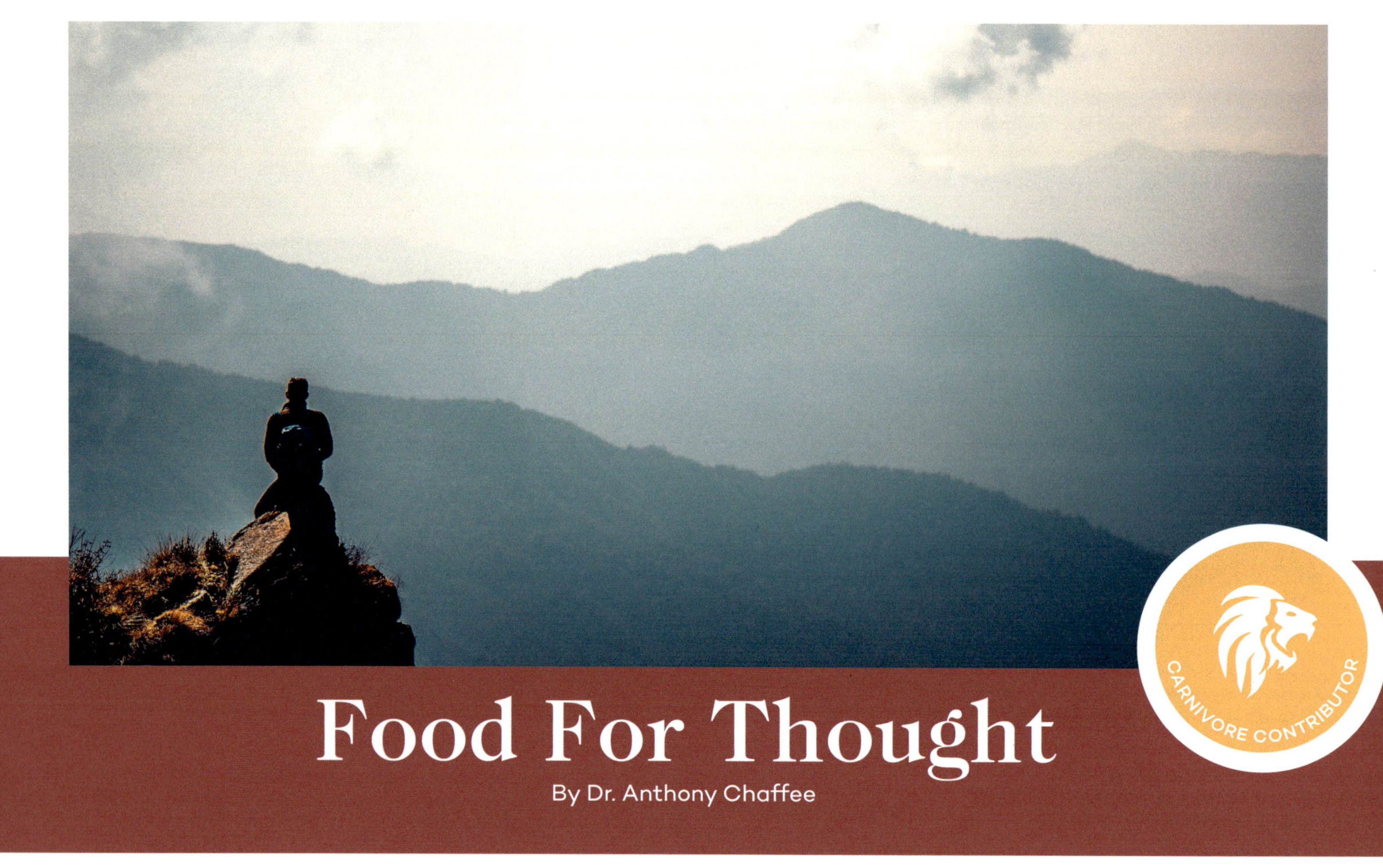

Food For Thought

By Dr. Anthony Chaffee

In 1977 the USDA proclaimed that saturated fat and cholesterol cause heart disease and a host of other diseases, now shown to be based on fraudulent data used to cover up the real culprit, sugar. Or more specifically, fructose. **Since then, we've reduced our fat and red meat intake by 30%, and yet all of the diseases claimed to be caused by excess fat intake increased dramatically.** Cardiovascular disease rates tripled, the obesity rate tripled, and even cancer rates have tripled. Autoimmune diseases have shot up as well. Type 2 diabetes rates have increased exponentially and now accounts for around two-thirds of the Medicare and Medicaid budget every year, with only 9% of the population diabetic and 40% of population pre-diabetic. Think about that for a second, and what that will mean for our population's health and our health care budget and spending if this trajectory isn't altered.

What else increased at that exact same time? One was **dementia,** which recent studies show can be protected against by having high LDL cholesterol, the so-called bad cholesterol, and a diet high in saturated fats. This is because, in my opinion, we dramatically reduced or even removed our only source of essential fatty acids among other nutrients that are used to build and repair the brain and it's structures, especially in the elderly population who almost always have some sort of heart condition for which they are put on a low fat, "heart healthy" diet, and replaced them with processed carbohydrates.

There's something else that people don't realize: **Autism also increased dramatically** at this same time. Now there are studies that suggest certain diets such as vegetarianism may exclude certain nutrients that are necessary for proper development and could lead to Autism. And some of these studies are causitive, not correlative. Texas A&M University has shown causation between a vegetarian and vegan diet with a certain form of autism due to a carnitine deficiency. Quarantine is not found in plants or fungi, and some people don't make enough of it naturally so they need it in their diet to form normal functioning neurons. We also see that certain preconception diets protect against Autism. Of the 14 foods found to be protective, 12 are meat or animal based. Also of interest, children with autism have been reducing their symptoms by removing grains and other carbohydrates, as well as sugar. It is my suggestion and opinion that this autism upswing is a direct cause of removing healthy meat and animal fat from our diet and replacing it with sugars and plant based carbohydrates.

It seems funny to me that people will look at the research and evidence showing that fat was used as a scapegoat for sugar back in the 1980s and agree that fat was never the problem, and yet they will still avoid fat in their diet and in the diets of their children. At the same time, they will also give their kids candy and sugar-filled treats, even though fructose is metabolized into the exact same byproducts as ethanol, so it's literally like giving your kid a couple shots of whiskey per can of soda. People need to look past everything they've been told growing up to see the evidence at hand, especially when that evidence could save their kids from getting autism and a whole host of other chronic diseases.

"People need to look past everything they've been told growing up to see the evidence at hand"

That is why I promote a carnivore diet, because food is species specific and when you dabble in the Plant and Fungi Kingdoms you will get a host of defense chemicals and protections that those plants and fungi use to stop animals like us from eating them. That's Botany 101, and a hard fact from one of the few hard sciences.

Whether or not you believe the evidence that humans are carnivores biologically, which I think it overwhelmingly does, no animal on earth eats such a wide variety of plant-based foods as we do in a daily basis. Animals in the wild eat a very specific, monotonous diet and if they consist of plants at all they consist of a very limited variety. One thing you can be sure of on a carnivore diet is that it does eliminate out all of the plants and processed ingredients that are certainly not biologically appropriate for us, if any are, which contain many harmful agents that can and do cause harm.

The massive increase in disease prevalence since we've changed our diet as a people, along with biological, botanical, and biochemical evidence, and countless studies and randomized controlled trials in the literature, leads me to the conclusion that the so-called chronic diseases that we treat today as a mainstay of modern medicine are not diseases per se but toxicities and malnutrition: toxic buildup of a species inappropriate diet and a lack of species specific nutrition. Namely, too many plants and not enough healthy, fatty meat.

This is clearly demonstrated by the fact that these so-called diseases can be reversed when you remove these harmful "foods." In the case of autoimmune diseases for instance, putting people on an elemental diet, providing only the nutrients required for life and nothing else, this is a better treatment for flare ups of Crohn's disease than steroids. In a controlled trial, by going on a low fiber ketogenic diet, versus a diet rich in carbohydrates and fiber, the ketogenic group kept Crohn's patients in remission an average of 51 weeks, while the control group with carbohydrates and fiber kept them in remission an average of 0 weeks. That's not a lot of weeks. Researchers such as Professor Steve Phinney have shown with large trials that type 2 diabetes is ultimately reversible with the simple elimination of carbohydrates, sugar, and alcohol. It may not be easy, but it is simple. On the topic of ketogenic diets, another study found that the removal showed better efficacy for treating Alzheimer's than every single pharmaceutical agent ever even trialled. Changing what someone eats can change everything.

These are but a few small examples, but there are many more already available in the literature, with mounting supportive evidence showing the reversible nature of these diseases. Institutions and clinicians have already taken these dietary measures on board to treat their patients and reverse these diseases first hand, myself included. Even such major institutions as Cedars-Sinai Medical Center has taken to using ketogenic metabolic therapy to treat cancer patients.

And let's not forget the recent study from Harvard with 2,000 people who have gone carnivore and significantly improved their health and reversed many diseases. That, like most epidemiology in nutrition, is a good starting point that will hopefully encourage new, larger and more rigorous trials to show once and for all the benefits of going back to our roots and eating as we are biologically designed to eat: as Carnivores.

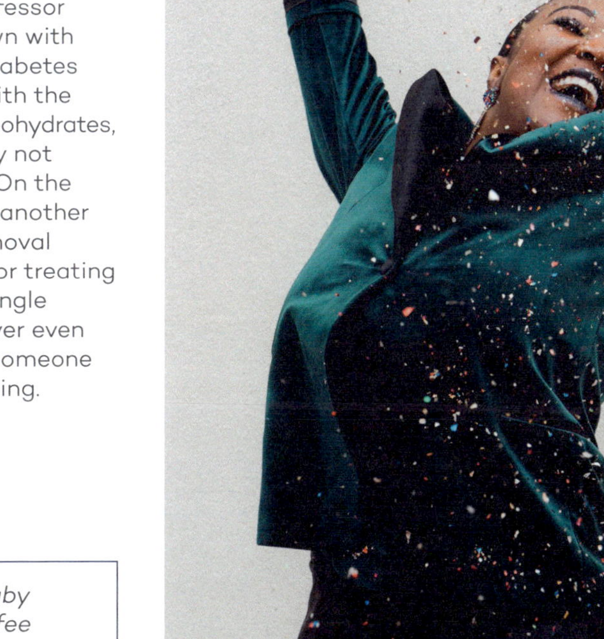

Dr. Anthony Chaffee is a medical doctor, former professional rugby player, and the host of 'The Plant Free MD' podcast. Dr. Chaffee helps clients shed weight, optimize their health, and revitalize their lives through incorporating the Carnivore diet and other lifestyle changes with scientifically supported methods.

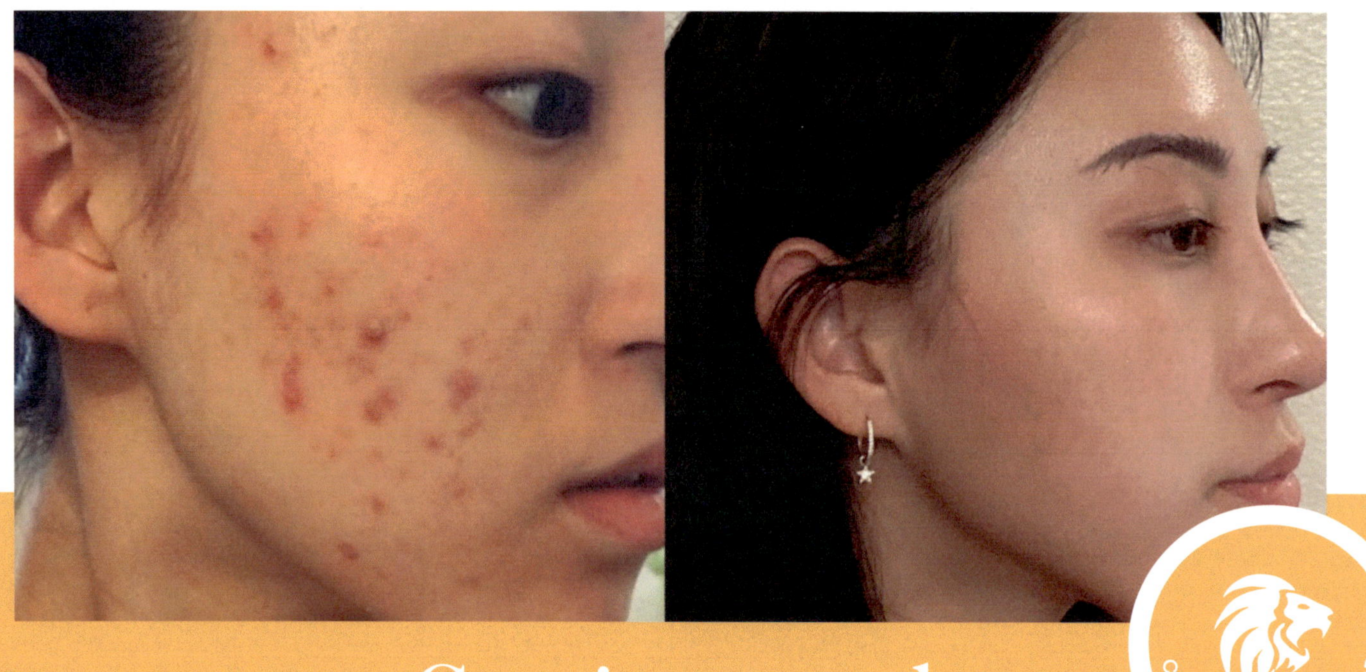

Carnivore and Skin Conditions

By Bella the Steak and Butter Gal

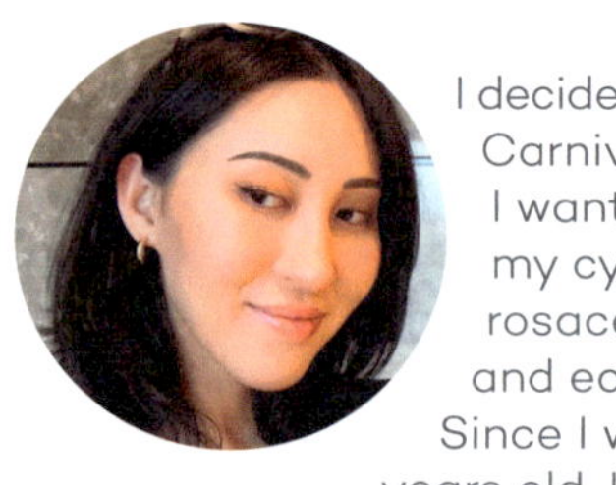

I decided to go Carnivore because I wanted to heal my cystic acne, rosacea, psoriasis, and eczema. Since I was 14 years old, I suffered with these skin issues and as a result, had low self-esteem because of how ashamed I felt about the appearance of my skin. I remember caking on layers and layers of concealer and avoiding harsh direct light so that no one had to see the bumps and texture of my inflamed skin. On top of that, I started to become more self conscious of my weight and even fell into the trap of believing that "eating fat makes you fat". I eventually went on the vegan diet to hopefully lose weight and improve my skin but that only led to my health declining even more. Eating a high carb low fat plant-based diet eventually caused me to lose my period and I suffered from amenorrhea for 2 years before I finally realized the obvious: My diet was clearly lacking in the nutrition my body needed to function optimally. It was actually my own doctor who suggested that I start eating animal foods if I wanted to improve my health! That day was a wake up call for me and I remember going home and searching on my laptop for anything I could find about vegans going back to eating meat. I was pleasantly surprised by how many videos and articles popped up including videos of vegans going carnivore like Kasumi Kriss and Asra Conlu. Their healing stories inspired me so much that **I started researching more on the Carnivore Die**t and that is how I came across OG's like Dr. Shawn Baker, Jordan Peterson and Mikhaila Peterson, Kelly Hogan, and Dr. Ken Berry.

After devouring all the carnivore interviews and content available at that time, I started the Carnivore Diet on January 1st of 2019.

From that day forward, I began my healing journey and now 4 years into it, I have fully reversed my autoimmune skin disorders AND regained a healthy painless cycle. My psoriasis and eczema are gone, my cystic acne breakouts no longer occur, and I no longer feel the need to cover my face with layers of makeup. If I can share my best tip from my experience so far, it is to not fear the fat!! Eating butter and fatty meat every single day has truly changed my life and I would not have the results and benefits I have today, without these foods.

Bella is a 3-year carnivore influencer who has amassed large followings on YouTube and Instagram. She is the founder of the Steak and Butter Gang. The Steak and Butter Gang is a private support community of carnivores, ketovores, and carni-curious people who are seeking guidance, accountability, and motivation to conquer their health and weight loss goals.

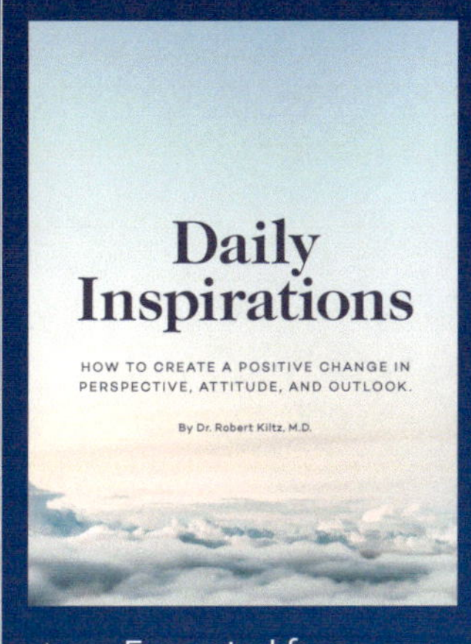

Excerpted from
DAILY INSPIRATIONS
by Dr. Robert Kiltz, MD

It's a Beautiful Day

We often wake up, brush our teeth, hurry out the door and go about our daily activities without being aware of the magic that surrounds us. We forget to breathe the fresh air into our lungs from our universe, smile at the sky and the clouds, feel the sun warm on our face, and truly marvel at the wonders of our surroundings. Everything we see, touch and feel comes from energy. Everything around us once began as energy. It is important that we feel the energy from our environment and allow it to flow through our bodies. We are created from the same energy from which the sky, soil, and water was born.

When we become aware of our surroundings out in the world, we feel connected to our universe and feel a sense of "oneness" with nature. Using our senses to guide us, we begin to see the beauty in each day and look at the gifts nature has bestowed upon us with new eyes and appreciation. A tree that you see every single day may look completely differen with this new awareness.

"Looking for and enjoying beauty is a way to nourish the soul. The universe is in the habit of making beauty. There are flowers and songs, snowflakes and smiles, acts of great courage, laughter between friends, a job well done, the smell of fresh-baked bread. Beauty is everywhere."

— Matthew Fox

Carnivore Resources:

Great minds! Dr. Kiltz has interviewed or been interviewed by many of the top Carnivore thinkers. Lots of great videos to watch and information and tips to absorb.

KELLY HOGAN

Instagram: @kelly_hogan91

YouTube Handle: @myzerocarblife

BRIAN SANDERS

Website: nosetotail.org

Instagram: @foodlies & @eatnosetail

AMBER WENTWORTH

Website: Lone-Star-Keto.com

Instagram: @lonestarketogirl

Youtube: Lone Star Keto

Facebook: @lonestarketogirl

Twitter: @lone_star_keto

DR. SARAH ZALDIVAR

Website: https://drsarahzaldivar.com/

UDEMY instructor page: https://www.udemy.com/user/sarah-zaldivar/

Instagram: https://www.instagram.com/cnyfertility/

YouTube: https://www.youtube.com/channel/UCBXm-oCTN-dJdbD65gK5IEQ

Facebook: https://www.facebook.com/drsarahzaldivar/

Twitter: https://twitter.com/DrSarahZaldivar

DR. GARY FETTKE

Website: lowcarbdownunder.com.au

YouTube: Low Carb Down Under

Twitter: @FructoseNo

Instagram: @isupportgary

DR. TRO KALAYJIAN

Website: doctortro.com

Podcast: https://podcasts.apple.com/us/podcast/low-carb-md-podcast/id1441557261

Instagram: https://www.instagram.com/doctortro/

Twitter: https://twitter.com/DoctorTro

Facebook: https://www.facebook.com/DoctorTro/

Youtube: https://www.youtube.com/channel/UCCZoglf1EL7upJgmb_KaFLQ

DR. ANTHONY CHAFFEE

Instagram: @anthonychaffeemd

Podcast: "The Plant Free MD

SHAWN BAKER, MD -

Amazon best-selling author of The Carnivore Diet

Website: https://carnivore.diet/dr-shawn-baker-md/

Instagram: @shawnbaker1967

YouTube: Dr. Shawn Baker

Podcast: Revero Podcast

Carnivore Resources:

ALEXIS COLANTONIO

Website: purenaturalkitchen.com

Website: purenaturalmind.com

Instagram: @purenaturalkitchen

Facebook: @purenaturalliving

Twitter: @purenaturallife

DR. JAIME SEEMAN

Website: .doctorfitandfabulous.com

Instagram: @doctorfitandfabulous

YouTube: Doctor Fit and Fabulous

Podcast: humanperformanceoutliers.libsyn.com/

ZACH BITTER

Website: https://zachbitter.com/

Instagram: @ZachBitter

Podcast websites: https://zachbitter.com/hpo

BELLA

Website: https://sbg-s-meat-up.mn.co/

Youtube: Steak and Butter Gal

Instagram: @steakandbuttergal

JUDY CHO

Website: https://nutritionwithjudy.com/

Instagram: @nutritionwithjudy

ROBERT ORION SIKES

Website: https://ketosavage.com/

AUSTIN CAVELLI, MS, PA-C

Website: QualityCarnivore.com

Instagram: @qualitycarnivore

Facebook: qualitycarnivore

YouTube: Quality Carnivore

PAUL SALADINO

Website: https://carnivoremd.com

Instagram: carnivoremd2.0

Podcast: https://carnivoremd.com/category/podcasts/

DR. KEN BERRY

Website: drberry.com

Instagram: KenDBerryMD

Facebook: KenDBerryMD

MARIA EMMERICH

Website: mariamindbodyhealth.com

Instagram: mariaemmerich

Vimeo: Maria Emmerich

Quality Meat Suppliers:

Snake River Farms

My go-to steak. A bit pricey, but nothing beats the incredible American wagyu of snake river farms shipped right to your door.

snakeriverfarms.com

Butcher Box

There's nothing like the convenience of subscription grass fed, grass finished beef and other meat products. My go to for mouth watering meats!

butcherbox.com

Nose to Tail

Founded by my friend and carnivore thought leader Brian Sanders, Nose to Tail offers amazing fresh meats, beef snacks, animal-based soaps/lotions and so much more.

nosetotail.org/

Hudson Valley Foie Gras

You can't beat Hudson Valley for delicious foie gras or duck fat. Their cage-free, responsibly raised ducks provide unbeatable flavor and nutrition.

hudsonvalleyfoiegras.com

Carnivore Crips

I'm usually a leftover steak in a Ziploc bag kind of guy if I need a snack or am on the road, but these crunchy yummy and nutritious snacks are well worth it!

carnivorecrisps.com

First Light Farms

Grass-fed wagyu and venison right to your door. Yup, it's damn good stuff!

firstlight.farm

US Wellness Meats

My go-to steak. A bit pricey, but nothing beats the incredible American wagyu of snake river farms shipped right to your door.

grasslandbeef.com

Alpine Butcher

Online Butcher Offering USDA Prime Hand Cut Steaks For Home Delivery

alpinebutchershop.com

Porter Road

Great high-quality meat shipped right to your door.

porterroad.com/

Eat Meat, Live Longer

Australian study finds eating meat correlates to a longer life expectancy

A biomedicine researcher from the University of Adelaide in Australia examined meat consumption in more than 170 countries. Research found a meat-based diet correlates to greater life expectancy, independent of total calorie intake, economic affluence, urban advantages, and obesity. It also revealed energy from carbohydrate crops (grains and tubers), prevalent in vegan or vegetarian based diets, does not lead to longer life expectancy. Steak anyone?

The Gratitude Attitude

There's no better way to set the tone for your day by waking up and greeting the day "Thank you, God, for this awesome and amazing day you have gifted me." This is how I start my day every day. I speak these words out loud and my day begins from there.

Gratitude has been found to be one of the strongest positive emotions and is often linked to happiness. Most of us are confused when it comes to gratitude. We think we need to achieve certain goals or get to a certain place in our lives before we take a breath and express appreciation for all that we have. In fact, happiness isn't what brings you gratitude, gratitude is what brings you happiness!

Some people find it helpful to make gratitude part of their family dinner, going around the table with each person sharing something good that happened to them that day and/or why they are thankful.

Teaching the next generation that there is good in every day is an important lesson to pass along and will be the building blocks for happiness.

Gratitude has physical, psychological, and social benefits. The practice of gratitude has been shown to improve your immune system, regulate blood pressure, reduce aches and pains, and help with sleep. Gratitude can help achieve higher levels of joy and allows those who practice it to feel less lonely and more optimistic.

The mind-body connection is very real and should not be ignored when it comes to health and wellness.

Part of the gratitude attitude is being kind to others and to yourself. I firmly believe that kindness begins with the person in the mirror. Make sure you are saying positive and uplifting things to yourself when you look in the mirror. **Love thyself first.**

"Thank you, God, for
this awesome and
amazing day you have
gifted me."

Nourish Your Mind & Feed Your Soul

As medical professionals, we spend a lot of talking about what you should be eating or what medicines you should be taking (as few as possible), but not as much time discussing how important what you put into your mind is as well.

I've spent a lot of time reading the works of great philosophers and spiritual leaders, both past and present, and can tell you that the phrase "food for thought" hits the mark. As much as you worry about what and how you to eat, you need to think carefully about what you're listening to and reading. What are you filling your conscious and subconscious mind with every day? Is it positive, amazing things that expand your mind and make you feel good or negative self-thought that brings you down?

There are so many wonderful books out there and some really smart, insightful people to learn from. Learning is a life-long pursuit. It shouldn't stop the day you get your high school, college, grad school, or even medical school diploma. We all have lots to learn and that means making a concerted effort to expose yourself to ancient texts (the Bible, the Koran, the Bhagavad Gita), the writings of Buddha, Lao Tzu, and newer books by present-day thinkers who are inspired by ancient healers and philosophers.

Share what you're learning and thinking about. Whether it's a tweet, a vlog, a Facebook/Instagram post, or an email to friends. Pass along those surprising/insightful/moving "nuggets" that you're absorbing from whatever you're reading or listening to.

> *"What you put into your mind and your mouth matters most."*

SLOW IT DOWN & BREATHE!

Practice daily meditation, prayer, and visualization 3-6 times per day..

We need to slow it down and focus on the beauty of the universe and the creativity that we've all been given. The gift is life.

MEDITATIVE BREATHING:

5-6-7 Breathe in Through the Nose and Out Through the Smile

I do this meditative breathing practice several times a day. You breathe in through the nose for 5 seconds; you hold it for 6; and you breathe out through the mouth for 7. I say, "In through the nose, out through the smile."

You can practice this 24/7/365, anytime of the day or night. The 5-6-7 rule is a meditative practice. You don't need to be sitting in a lotus position or at an ashram or the yoga studio. Right where you're sitting, standing, lying, resting, or relaxing is just fine.

Just stop what you're doing and focus on your breathing and having a positive/loving thought.

Come visit **DoctorKiltz.com** for more inspiration and ideas on how you can take your health and wellness to the next level and improve your Mindy, Body, and Smile.

How are You Feeling?

IF YOU'RE FEELING BLOATED . . . EAT LIKE THE CARNIVORE YOU ARE.

Take a look at what and when you're eating. Fruits and vegetables have a lot of chemicals that cause G.I. problems. Even a "healthy" diet can leave you feeling less than your best.

I recommend a heavily carnivore ketogenic diet that includes a streamlined selection of fat-dense foods – bacon, eggs, butter, beef, ice cream (homemade with full-fat heavy cream and just a few grams of sugar), and salt (to help with fluid balance and mineral retention). I support vegans & vegetarians! I recommend they cook down vegetables and add fat to them. And eat less frequently: **FASTING IS LASTING!**

Scientifically speaking, we don't need to eat plants. Carbohydrates — found abundantly in plants — are the only non-essential macronutrient. This means fats and proteins are necessary for our bodies to survive, but we don't need carbohydrates in the same way.

IF YOU'RE FEELING "FOGGY" . . . SPACE OUT YOUR MEALS.

Intermittent feasting (commonly known as intermittent fasting) is an important practice for giving our body the time it needs to rest and digest between meals. I am a big proponent of eating one meal a day (OMAD) just before bedtime so that my body has time to process the food while it's resting while it's resting, and it reduces the carb load to the inner-body. **Spacing out meals can improve your memory and mental clarity, heart health, weight loss, and improve tissue health.**

IF YOU'RE FEELING UNMOTIVATED . . . SET A POSITIVE INTENTION EACH DAY.

You create the vision of your health and wellness in your mind, and then you make it happen. Setting a daily intention can be a significant first step toward a more positive outlook and life. Every morning I write down my positive intention for the day. Intentions are different than goals. They're internal motivators and inspiration for how you want to treat yourself and others and how you want to live your life.

IF YOU'RE FEELING STRESSED AND OVERWHELMED . . . FIND MOMENTS FOR MINDFUL MEDITATION.

I practice meditative breathing several times a day and recommend you do the same. I breathe in through the nose for 5 seconds; hold it for 6 seconds, and breathe out through the mouth slowly for 7 seconds. This practice helps slow down thoughts, let go of negativity, and calm the mind and body.

No preparation is required. You can sit wherever you are for just 3-5 minutes.

IF YOU'RE FEELING BORED . . . TRY SOMETHING NEW.

We should always be learning and experiencing new things. Learn to knit, paint, clog, belly dance, speak Italian, draw, arrange flowers, or cook a great meal. YouTube is filled with fabulous 'learn to' videos, and there are subscription services for everything under the sun. Never stop exploring the things that interest you.

IF YOU'RE FEELING UNINSPIRED . . . LOOK TO OTHERS FOR INSPIRATION.

There are so many wonderful books and podcasts. You can learn from great philosophers and some every day folks who've gone on to do some pretty amazing things. Listen to a podcast or read a book. You are as capable as any other human being. Your past doesn't matter, or your physical capabilities. **We are capable of shifting and creating and making change, building on the old and building anew. Don't forget to keep looking for inspiration. It's out there.**

IF YOU'RE FEELING DOWN . . . DON'T FORGET TO BE GRACIOUS.

It's hard to do when things aren't going your way, **but gratitude is a daily practice.** Kindness begins with the person you see in the mirror. **Practicing gratitude has been shown to positively impact your physical and mental health.**

IF YOU'RE THINKING ABOUT MAKING A CHANGE . . . DO IT!

Simple as that. Do your research, but then get going! As Yoda said, "Do or do not. There is no try."

Need more ideas about how to feel your best. Tune in to Dr. Kiltz's weekly Fireside Chat.

"Do. Or do not. There is no try."
— Master Yoda

Do Something New

CREATE, BUILD SOMETHING, MAKE SOME MISTAKES

Studies link being open to new experiences with lower levels of inflammation, increased oxytocin, serotonin, and reduced cortisol and epinephrine. Get out there and do something new. It will benefit your mind and your body. If you've wanted to learn how to paint, knit, make pottery, master calligraphy, write a poem, learn an instrument, plant a garden, go do it!

I took up flying and earned my pilot's license in my mid-50s. Talk about stepping out of your comfort zone! Hitting the skyways at 10,000 feet behind the yoke with just you and the clouds is literally out of most of our comfort zones, but it's tremendously empowering. I'm now certified to fly a jet. Dreams do build you! But trying something new doesn't have to be an expensive, dangerous new hobby. I'm not suggesting we all start free-climbing on weekends (although try it if it's always been your dream, just be safe and get the proper training!).

Trying something new doesn't have to be a grand gesture. It can be as simple as taking a new route on your drive home from work so that you see different landmarks along the way and you get a new perspective.

It can mean pushing yourself creatively. Write something every day. It doesn't have to be a three-act play or short story. It can just be a few words about your day in a journal that you keep by your bed. Put pen to paper and write-out in long hand a couple of sentences or helpful reminders to yourself about how you're feeling and your goals. Or keep a digital diary on your phone if you want to be more high-tech.

For me, painting, potting and poetry have always been a creative outlet. I started working with pottery when I was in high school. Mrs. Wong in my ceramics class in 10th grade at John Marshall High School in Los Angeles inspired me through pottery and clay. I enjoy working in my pottery studio making art and throwing on the wheel, making slab pieces and more. Small pieces and big pieces, medium pieces, and pieces that end up in the bucket or on the floor. I make lots of mistakes, but I take something and do it and then do it again. The beauty of clay is that it is actually re-useable and moldable and changeable. I guess it's kind of like the human being. It doesn't matter where you've been. It is possible to reshape yourself in a new way, and learn to do things differently. Tapping into that creative part of my brain does wonders for stress and helps me feel connected to a higher power and the bigger picture.

I've since learned to paint, make jewelry, be a physician and surgeon, and learn new ideas about health and wellness, but ultimately, **it comes down to sticking to the loving, living, and learning, always and every day.**

FERTILIZE THE UNIVERSE: MAKE SOME MISTAKES

Fear of failure shouldn't hold you back but inspire you! If you're not making mistakes, then you're not doing anything new. I like to say that mistakes are fertilizer. Fertilizer is a good for the soil. It gives renewed growing power and strength to the seedlings that grow out of it. Failure is much the same. Failing makes us stronger, smarter, and more driven. Instead of saying, "I failed," say "I fertilized." There's a lot more truth to the latter.

When I first took up painting, my daughter told me I wasn't very good (and frankly, she was right), but that didn't stop me from doing more art. I worked at it and over time saw great improvement and found much joy in the act of painting itself.

FIND INSPIRATION ANYWHERE & EVERYWHERE

I'm inspired by others. **That's really what life is all about: seeing inspiration in all things!** Whoever you're around, begin to learn and listen. If you want to learn to build and do something, spend time around those successful people who have learned to build and grow something. You are as capable as any other human being. Your past doesn't matter or your physical capabilities. Mentally we are all capable. All of us, in one way or another, are capable of shifting and creating and making change, building on the old and building anew.

Are You Getting Enough Sleep?

If you're like 35% of Americans, you're not getting enough rest. Between job stress, family stress, blue light, and occasional Netflix binge watching, more and more adults don't get the recommended 7-9 hours of sleep each night. We're trying to fit it all in, and our sleep suffers. Most people don't recognize the long-term effects of night after night, year after year of sleep deficiency. Many people cut their rest short to do something else they think is healthy—early morning exercise. **But getting less than about 6 hours of sleep has real heath consequences, including a higher risk for memory problems, obesity, heart disease, diabetes, infections, and depression. If you're focused on your health (and you should be), you need to make sleep a priority.**

- **GET ON A REGULAR SCHEDULE AND COMMIT TO A BEDTIME** that gives you 6+ hours of sleep. Work back from your wake-up time and stick to your plan! That means no late nights on weekends either. It's better for your body to maintain a consistent schedule 7 days a week. Big swings can make it difficult to fall sleep.

- **EMBRACE NAPS!** If you can't get to bed on time or get a bad night's sleep, going to bed earlier the next night isn't the fix. Fit in a short 20-30 minute nap, but make sure you do it before 4:00 pm or it will affect your ability to go to sleep at your regular bedtime.

- **PREPARE FOR BEDTIME.** Give your body and your mind time to wind down. Take a warm bath or shower. Dim the lights and stay off your tablet or laptop. A little yoga or stretching before bed is a great idea. Consider incorporating MEDITATION and PRAYER as part of your routine. Consider incorporating MEDITATION and PRAYER as part of your routine.

- **TURN OFF ALL ELECTRONICS 15-20 MINUTES PRIOR TO LIGHTS OUT.** It's a good idea to keep all electronics out of the bedroom to decrease temptation and eliminate interruptions.

- **INVEST IN YOUR SLEEP SPACE.** Buy a comfortable mattress, light blocking curtains or shades, comfortable sheets, and keep the thermostat low. Studies have found that the optimal temperature for sleep is quite cool, around 60° to 68° F. Temperatures in this range help to decrease core body temperature that in turn initiates sleepiness.

- **"EARLY TO BED, EARLY TO RISE, MAKES A MAN HEALTHY, WEALTHY, AND WISE."** It works! I am up at 4 am every day and in bed by 9 pm each night. I often nap between 1-3 pm for about 10-20 minutes. This is my meditative nap, and it gives me the physical, mental, and spiritual boost I need to finish my day.

Should I Go Dairy-Free?

Most of us lived through a childhood bombarded by commercials and jingles telling us to drink our milk and how good it was for our health and development. Remember the ad campaign where lots of famous people sported milk mustaches? "Milk, it does the body good" was a popular slogan, but does it?

Many people have trouble processing dairy. In fact, about 75% of the world's population suffers from lactose intolerance—a genetic inability to properly digest milk and other dairy products. Common sense would tell us this isn't surprising given that we are humans, NOT cows. What's more, between the ages of 2 and 5 (weaning age) , the majority of humans naturally stop producing lactase, the enzyme required to properly metabolize lactose—the sugar found in milk.

Some of us don't even know we have a dairy intolerance until we give it up for a period of time and are amazed at the changes we experience.

TRY IT AND SEE:

Try giving up all dairy. That means eliminating ALL milk, cheese, yogurt, and ice cream for two weeks and see if you feel better. You may notice improvements with your sinuses, post-nasal drip, headaches, irritable bowel syndrome, energy, and weight. Then start eating dairy again and see how you feel. If you feel worse, consider adopting a dairy-free diet.

While dairy products are a good source of protein and fat (especially full fat cream), they can be inflammatory to some. The decision to consume/not to consume dairy really must be made on an individual basis.

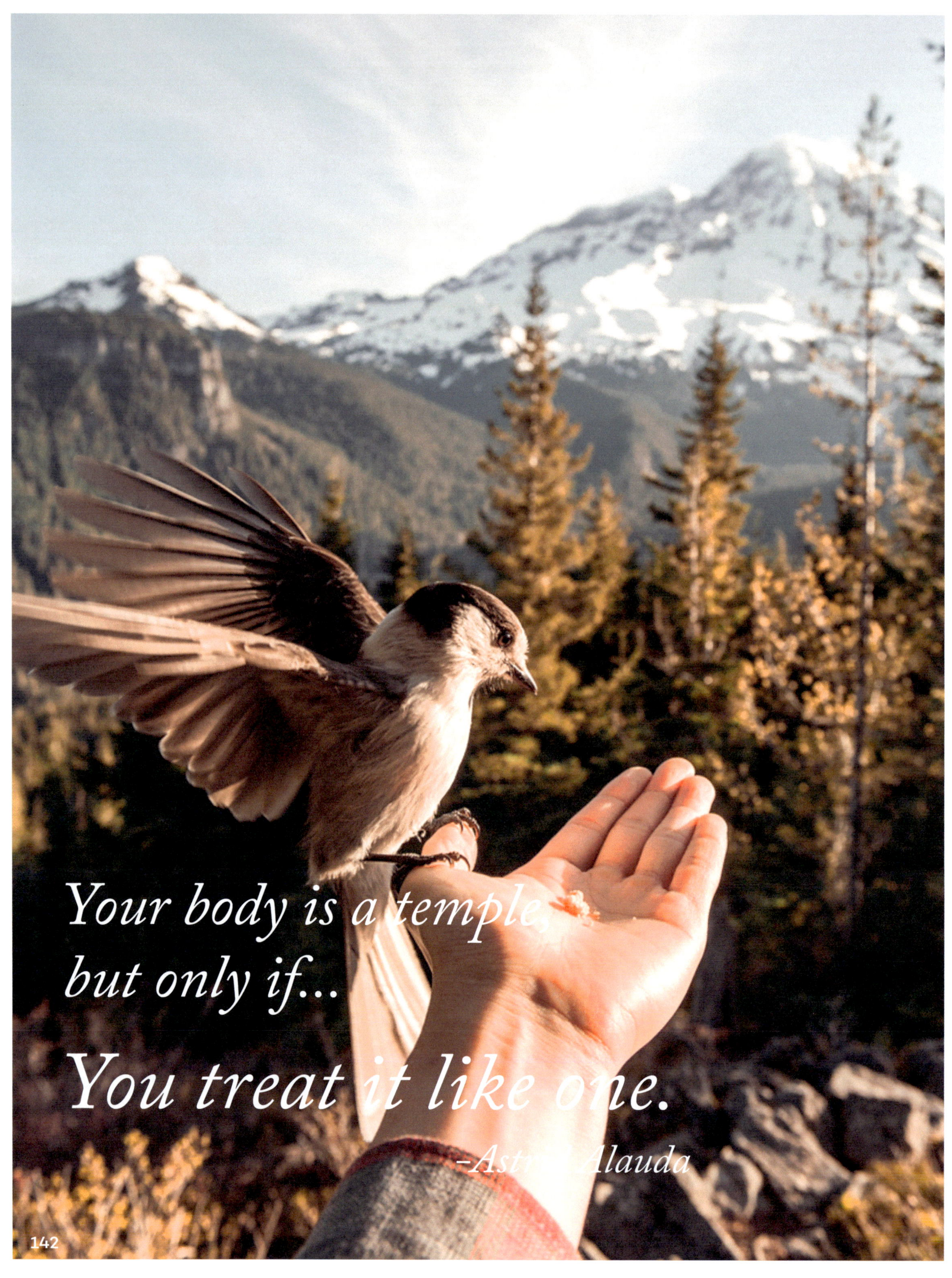
Your body is a temple,
but only if…
You treat it like one.
–Astrid Alauda

The Power of Laughter & Kindness

The act of laughing decreases the secretion of epinephrine and cortisol. It reduces stress, promotes relaxation, and improves circulation. Deep belly laughter is positively linked to the lymphatic and immune systems.

And if you're holding onto anger, the opposite is true. Just thinking about an angry situation from the past can cause a six-hour dip in levels of the antibody immunoglobulin A. These are the cells that form the first line of the defense against infection, thereby weakening the immune system, even in healthy people!

"One minute of anger weakens the immune system for 4–5 hours. One minute of laughter boosts the immune system for 24 hours."

Kiltz Cups

Each and every one of us is unique, just like my cups

How it works

Each and every Kiltz Cup is crafted with love and attention in Dr. Robert Kiltz's Pottery studio in beautiful Skaneateles, New York.

Select Your Size

We keep things simple. Kiltz Cups are crafted in two main but somewhat variable sizes: espresso and coffee. You choose.

We Ship You a Mystery Cup

After your purchase, Dr. Kiltz selects a unique cup just for you, packages it with love, and sends it on its way.

Happily Ever After

Once you receive your one of a kind cup, you'll live the rest of your life in utter bliss as you enjoy the elixirs of your choosing in a cup fit for a king or queen.

Shop at www.kiltzcups.com

Kiltz's Mighty Tribe Apparel

Shop at https://www.kiltzmightytribeshop.com/

Apparel sizes range from SMALL to 5XL.

Delivery is $4.99. Shipping takes 1-2 weeks because products are made to order.

Pay by credit card, PayPal, Afterpay, and Google Pay.

30-Day free return policy

"Once we make our decision, all things will come to us. Auspicious signs are not a superstition, but a confirmation. They are a response."

— Deng Ming-Dao

Messages from the Universe

Throughout the duration of our lives, we are presented with gifts from the universe which come to us in the form of signs. These signs exist to help guide us through life harmoniously and to let us know when we are living according to our intended paths or when we're not. **When we are living the life that we are meant to live, the universe tells us that we are on the right path by smiling on us and giving us a sense of peace, tranquility, and happiness.**

We know we are living well because we feel we are living well. Things just flow effortlessly, nothing feels forced or pushed, and everything around us is in sync. When we are not living according to our intended path, the universe responds to this by sending us messages. Things become hard, painful, or don't seem to work the way we so desperately want them to. When this happens, instead of asking yourself "why me?" ask yourself instead "what can I do to shift my thoughts and actions to produce a different outcome?". Once you become aware of these gifts from the universe, you will begin to recognize them more readily and will be able to apply them to your life. Learning to acknowledge signs from the universe can be complicated at first, especially because the signs are not always as literal as we would like. Signs can take on many forms and can appear in a dream, on television, in an email, a conversation, or even an object in our home. We know that they are signs because we recognize them as such.

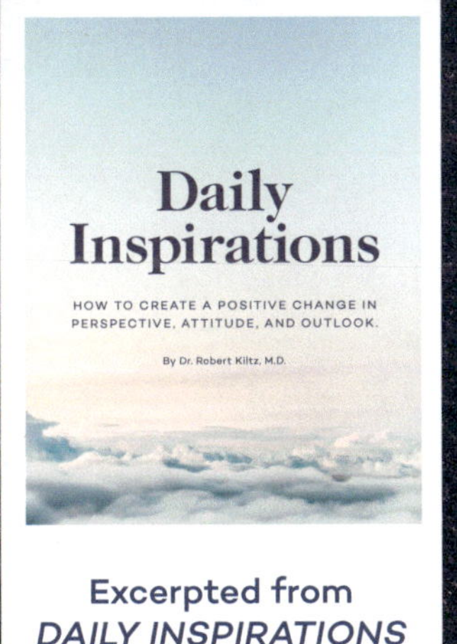

Excerpted from *DAILY INSPIRATIONS* by Dr. Robert Kiltz, MD

Dr. Kiltz's Learning Library

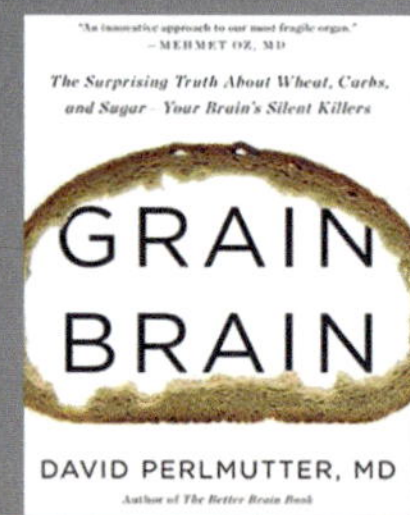

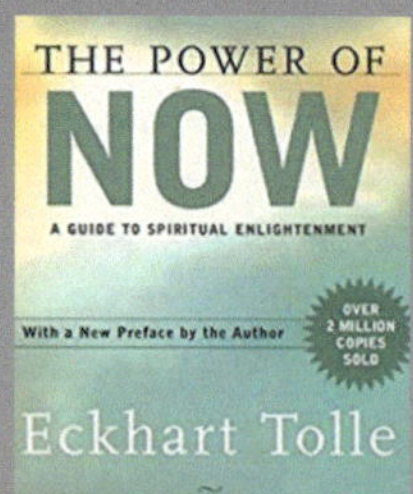

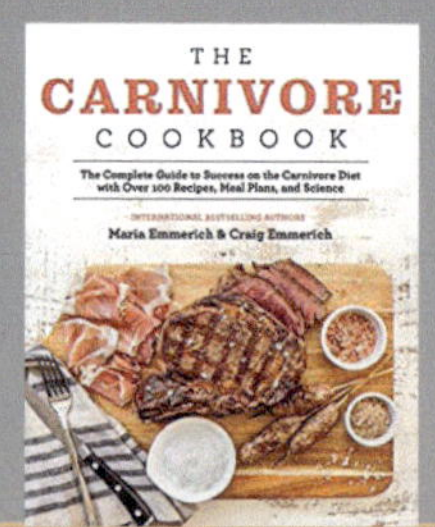

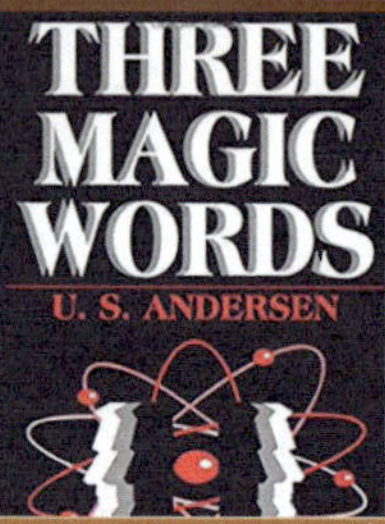

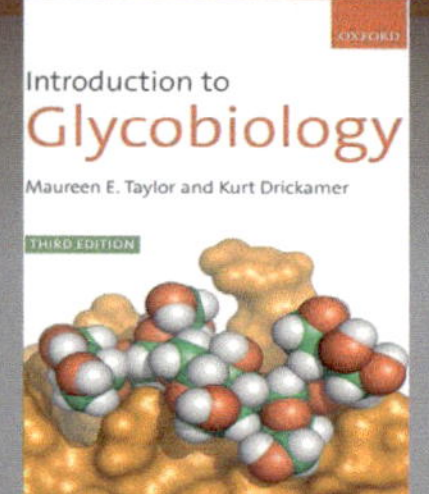

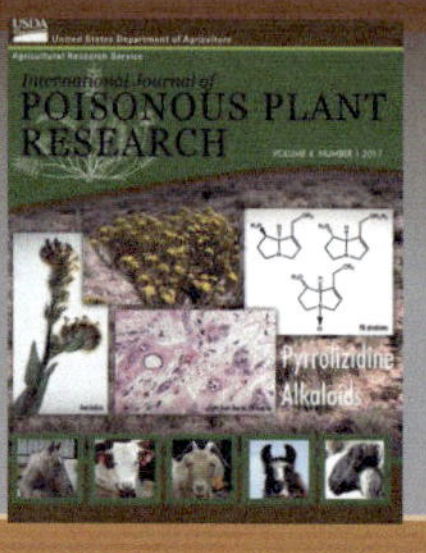

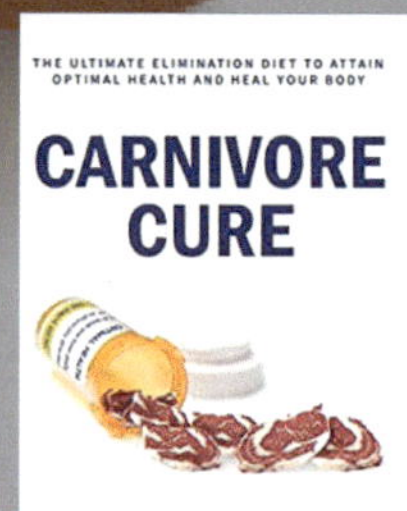

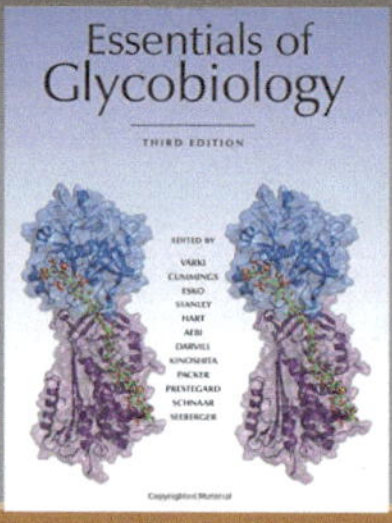

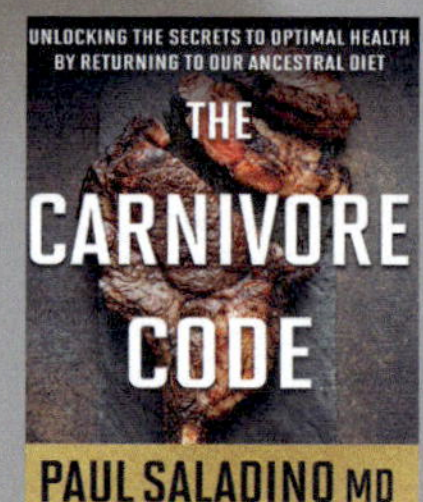

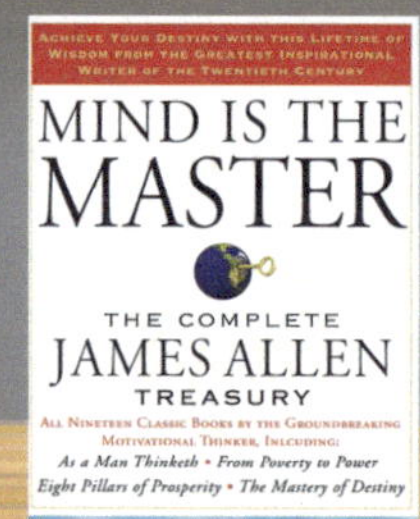

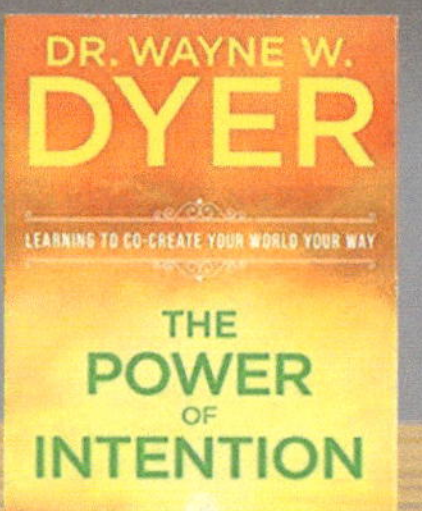

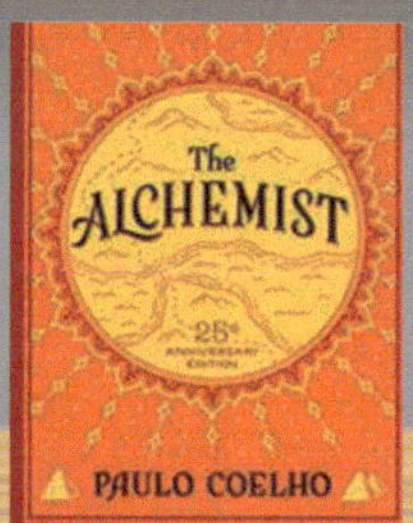

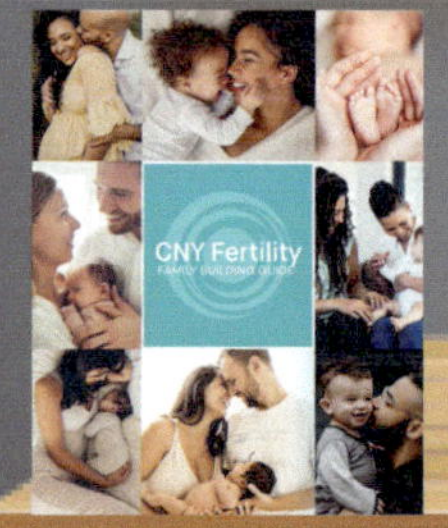

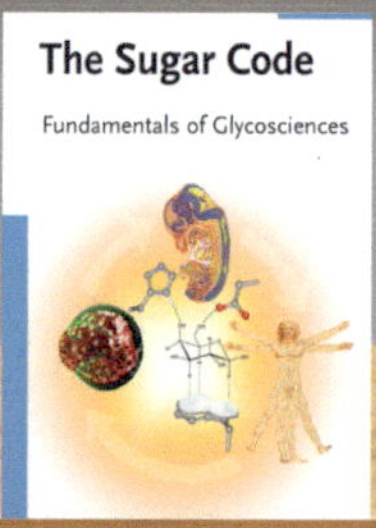

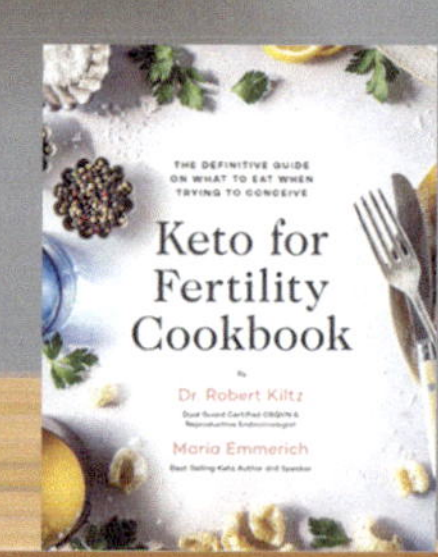

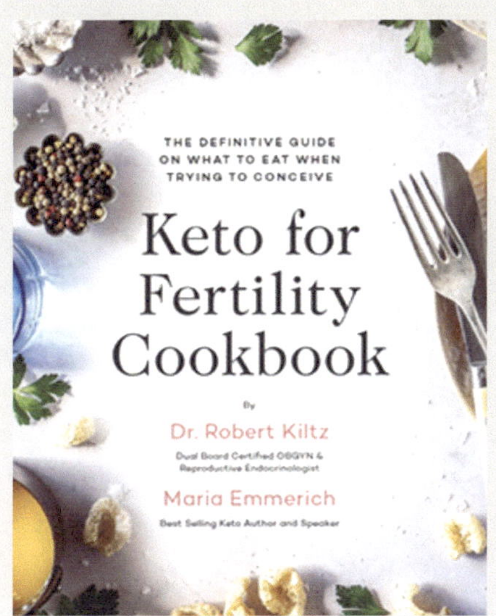

What do you get when a leading fertility expert and **a best-selling keto-expert/speaker** get together to write a cookbook that will help improve your fertility?

The Keto for Fertility Cookbook, that's what. Dr. Robert Kiltz and Maria Emmerich share the why, what, how, and when of eating to reduce inflammation and promote fertility when trying to conceive. This is a great introduction to the keto carnivore lifestyle and shares a carnivore heavy version of the keto diet.

Readers learn how a diet low in carbs, moderate in protein, and high in fat can **boost your fertility,** improving your overall health and odds of conception (with and without additional fertility assistance). Includes delicious, easy recipes and helpful tips to keep your pantry stocked with fertility-friendly ingredients. This HFLC (high-fat, low-carb) food plan has worked for patient after patient, even when modern fertility techniques failed.

Together, Dr. Kiltz and Maria Emmerich inspire a HFLC fertile lifestyle while guiding readers on the many ways it can improve how you feel, how you look, and ultimately your ability to conceive the child you've been longing for.

The Keto for Fertility Cookbook can be purchased in paperback or as an ebook at:

"Read, listen, or watch something positive every day. Get inspired!"

Made in United States
Cleveland, OH
02 January 2026